DOG WALKING COLORING BOOK

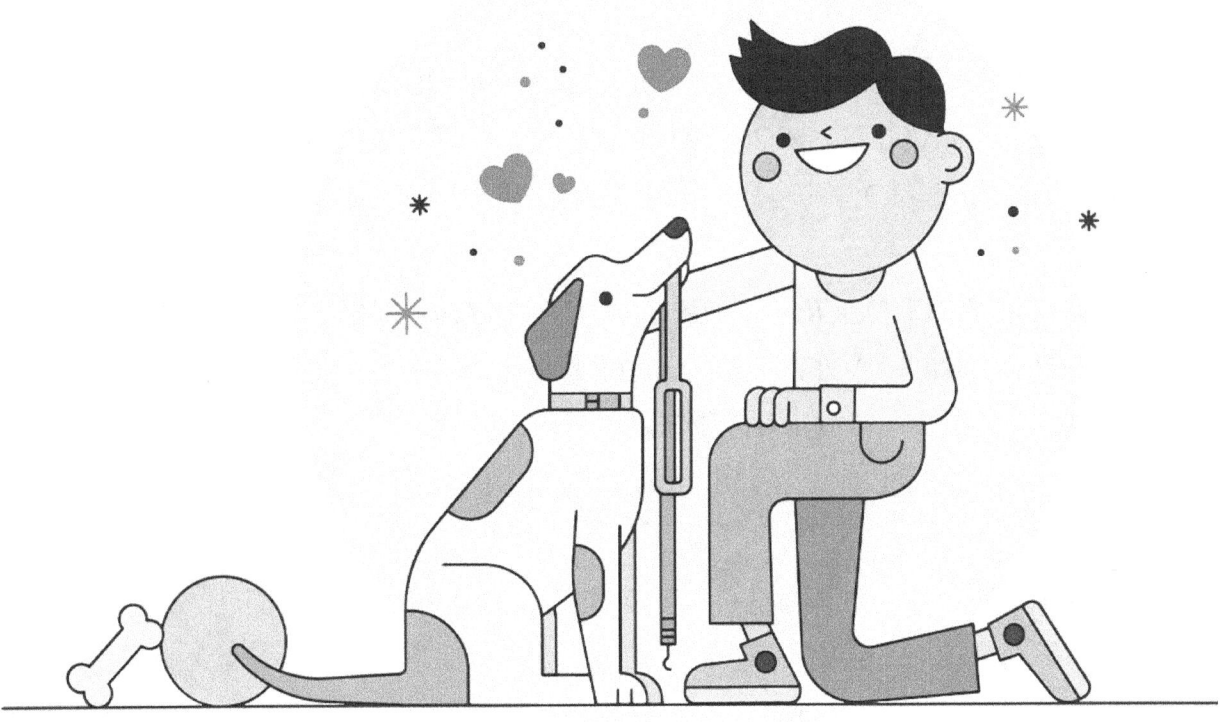

THIS COLORING BOOK BELONGS TO :

_____

_____

About This Dog Walking Coloring Book

Do you have a child that doesn't like to go dog walking with you?

Introduce dog walking to any children between 4 to 8 years old with this coloring book. Walking your dog is not just about potty breaks which kids might misunderstood. This activity helps a child develop themselves for socialization, sharing stories, physical exercise and learn how to handle animal like dog.

30 coloring pages in this book allows the child to paint their own story and let them use their imagination to tell you their story.
You will be surprised how creative a child can get.

Enjoy both coloring and dog walking together!

Hey! Thanks for purchasing this book and hope it helps you on your journey. All feedback on Amazon is greatly appreciated. We have put a lot of effort into this title, so if you are not completely satisfied email us at thechikkupublishing@gmail.com. You're also **INVITED** to receive a **Digital copy of 2021 Planner** at www.chikkupublishing.com

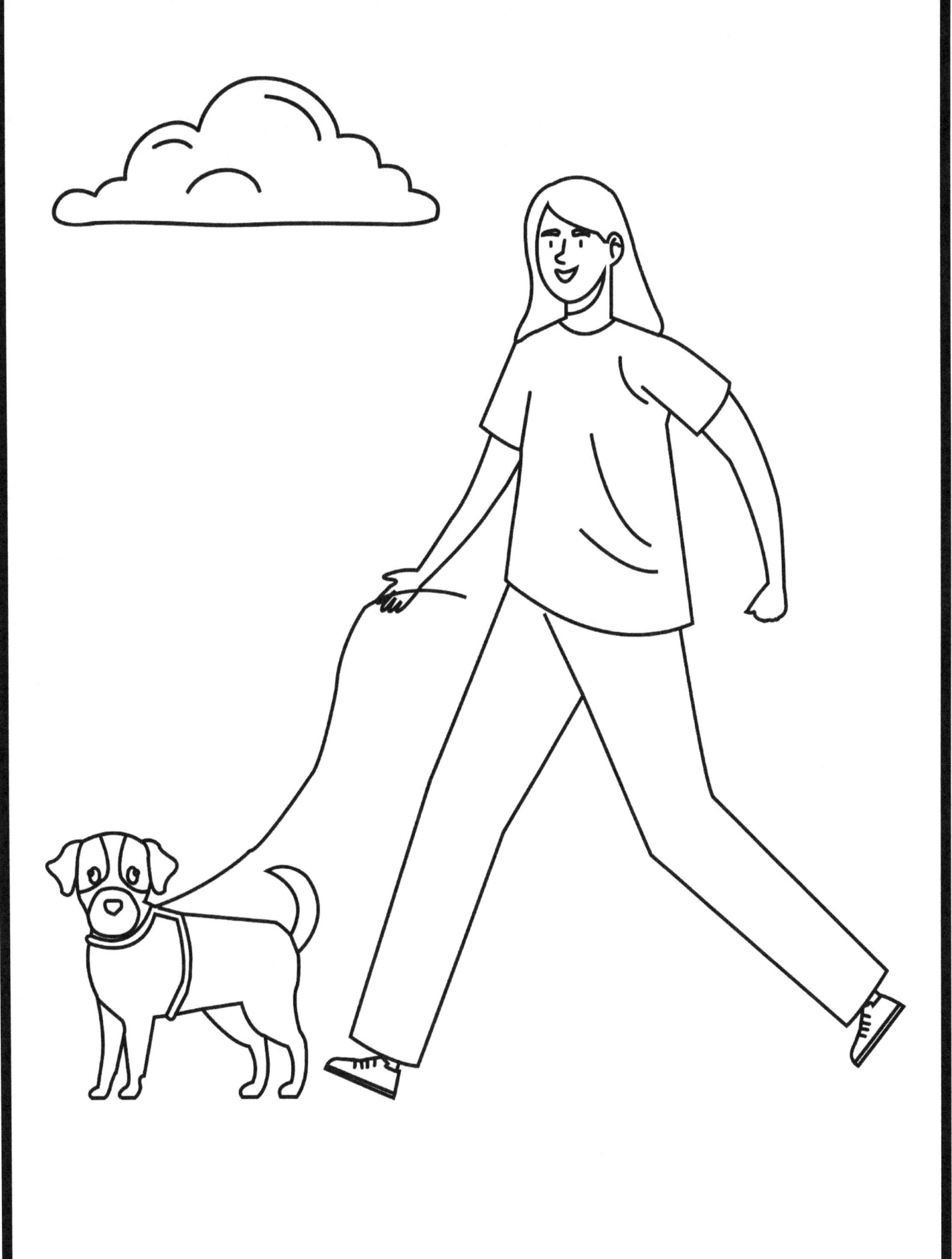

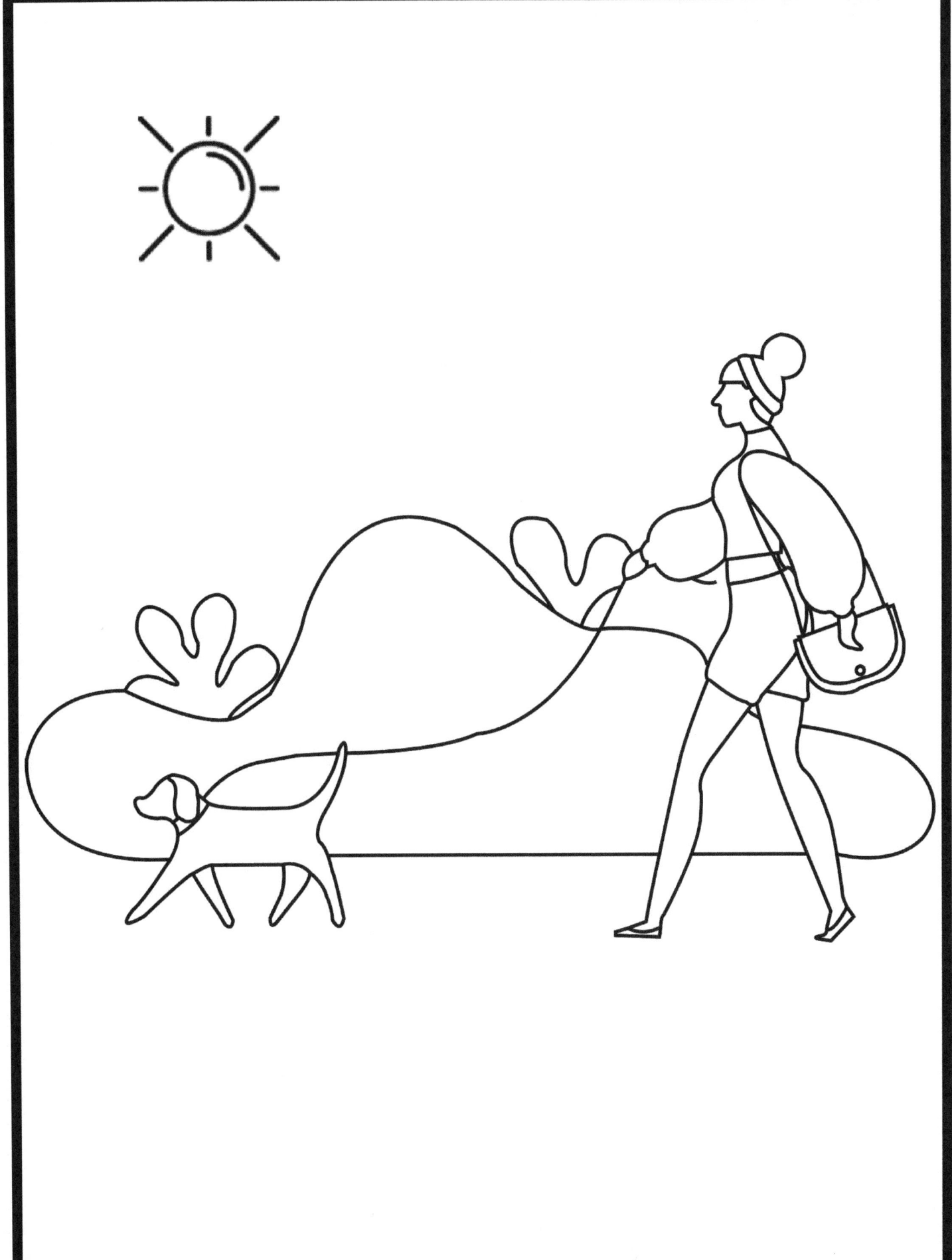

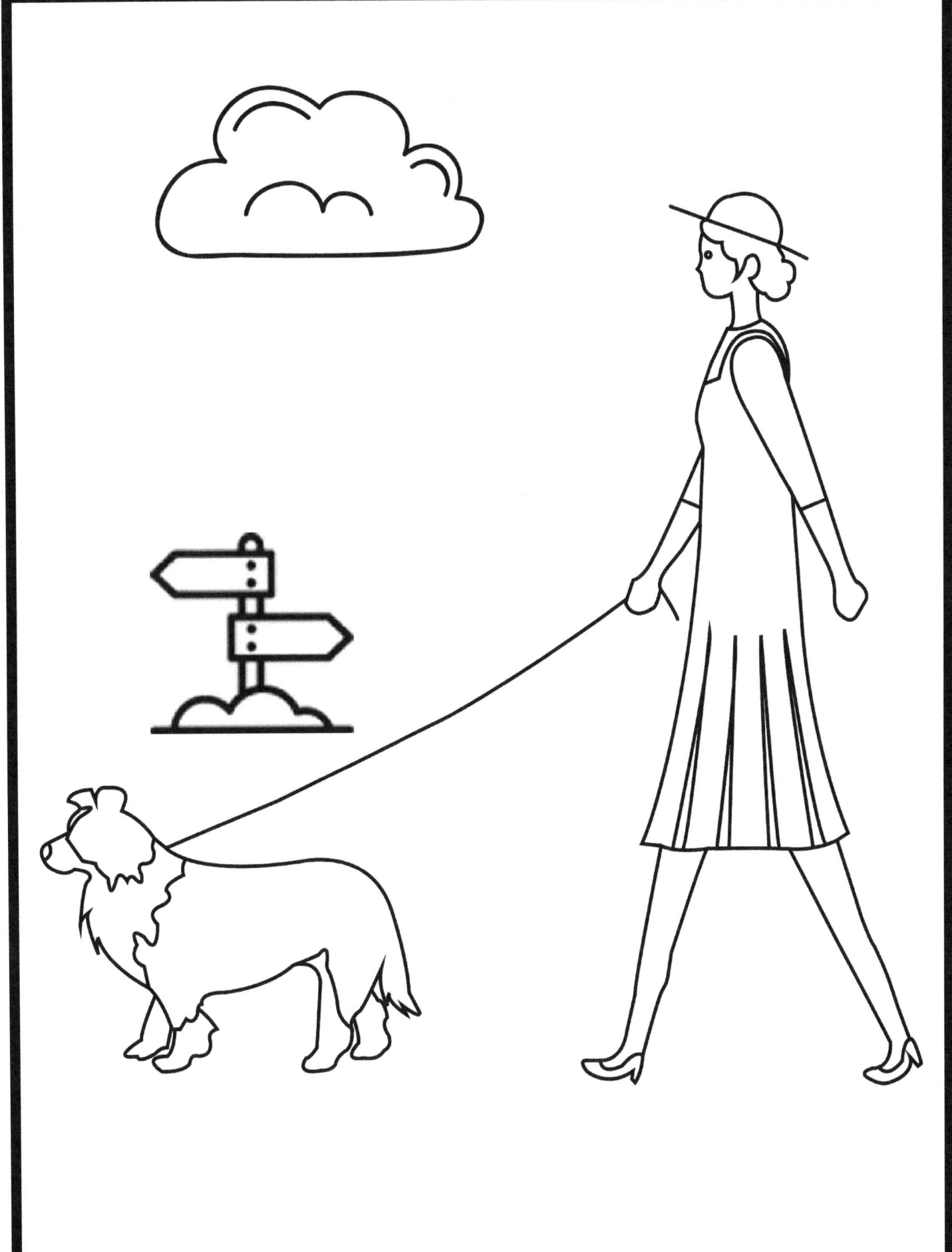

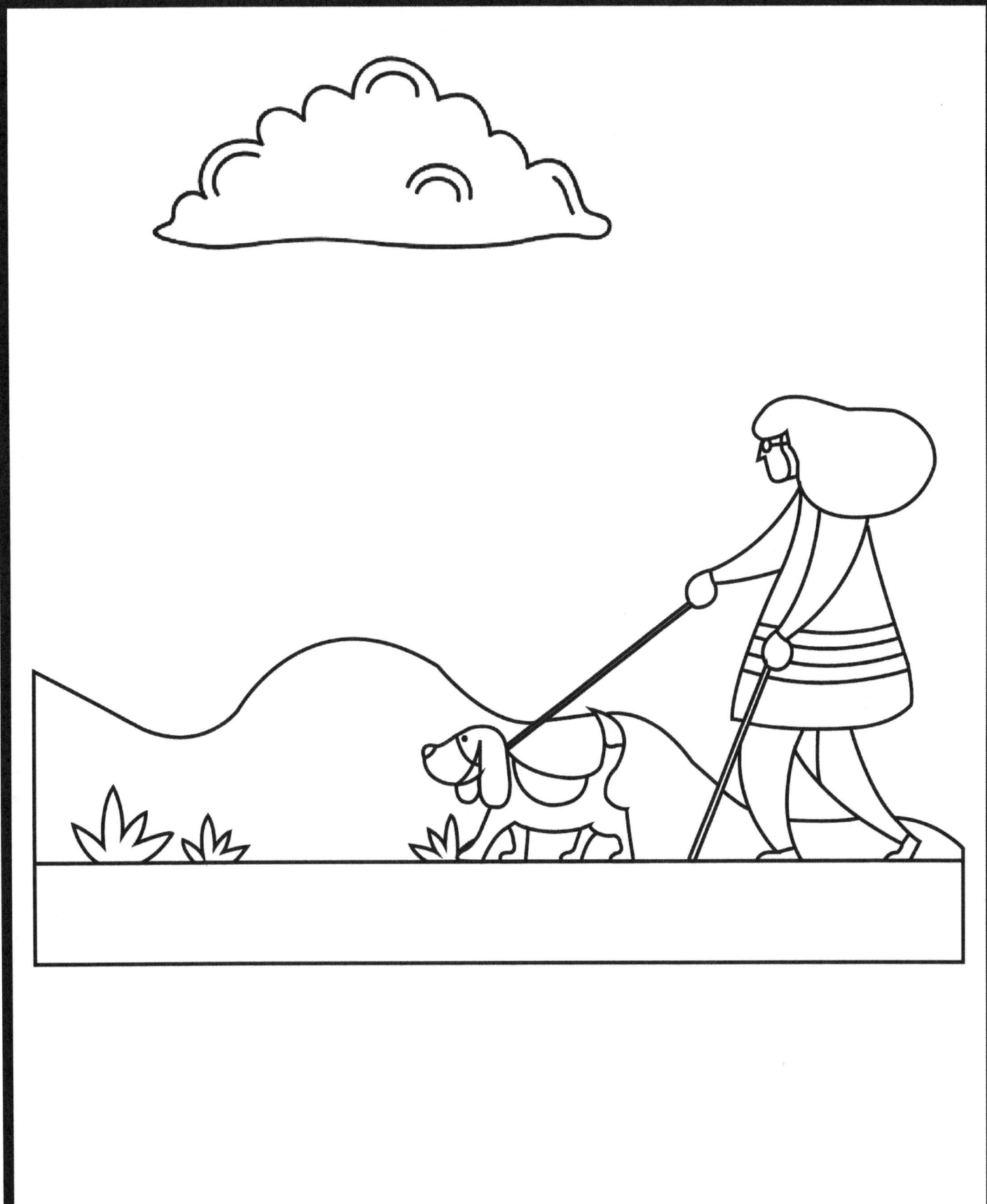

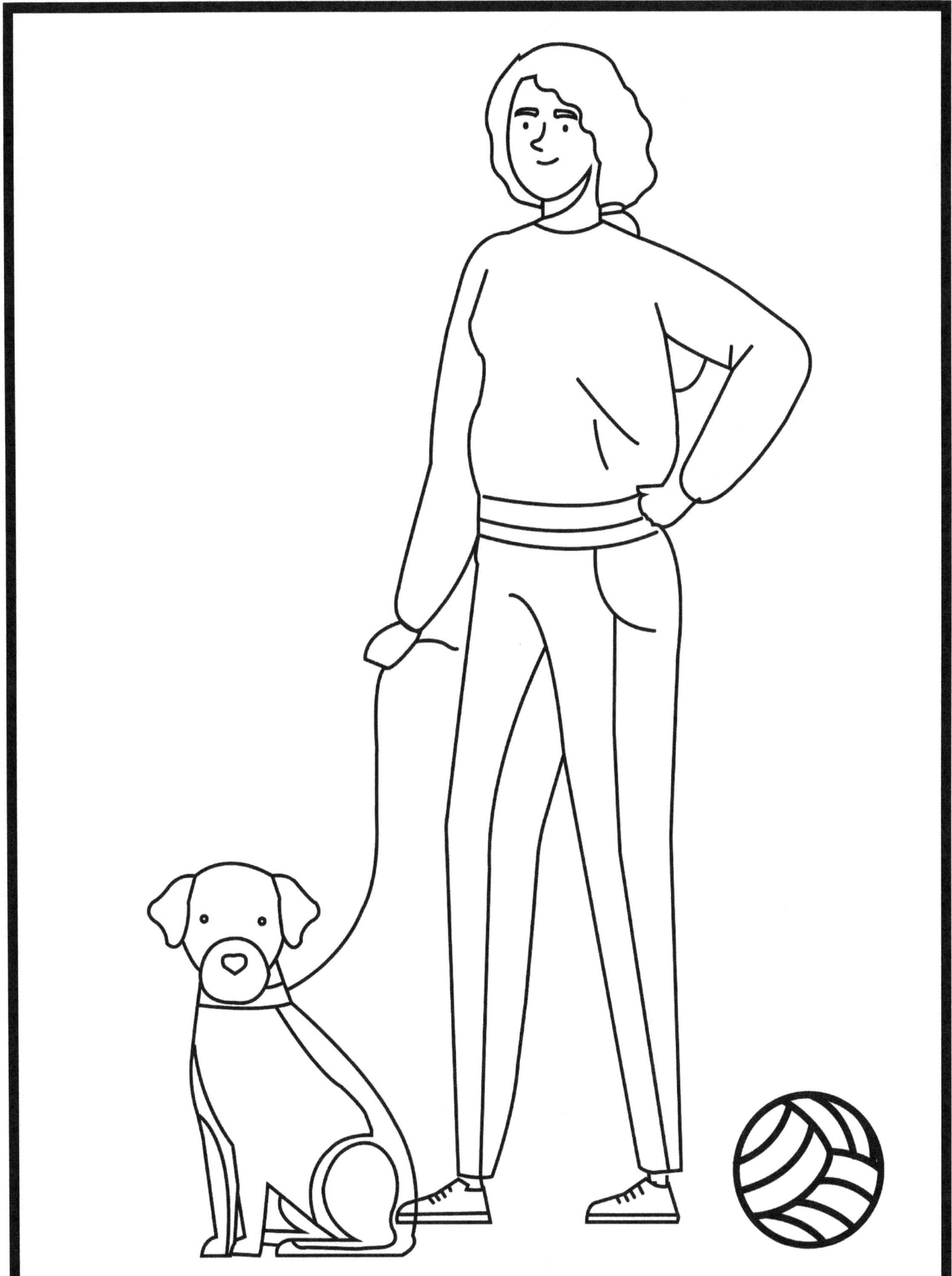

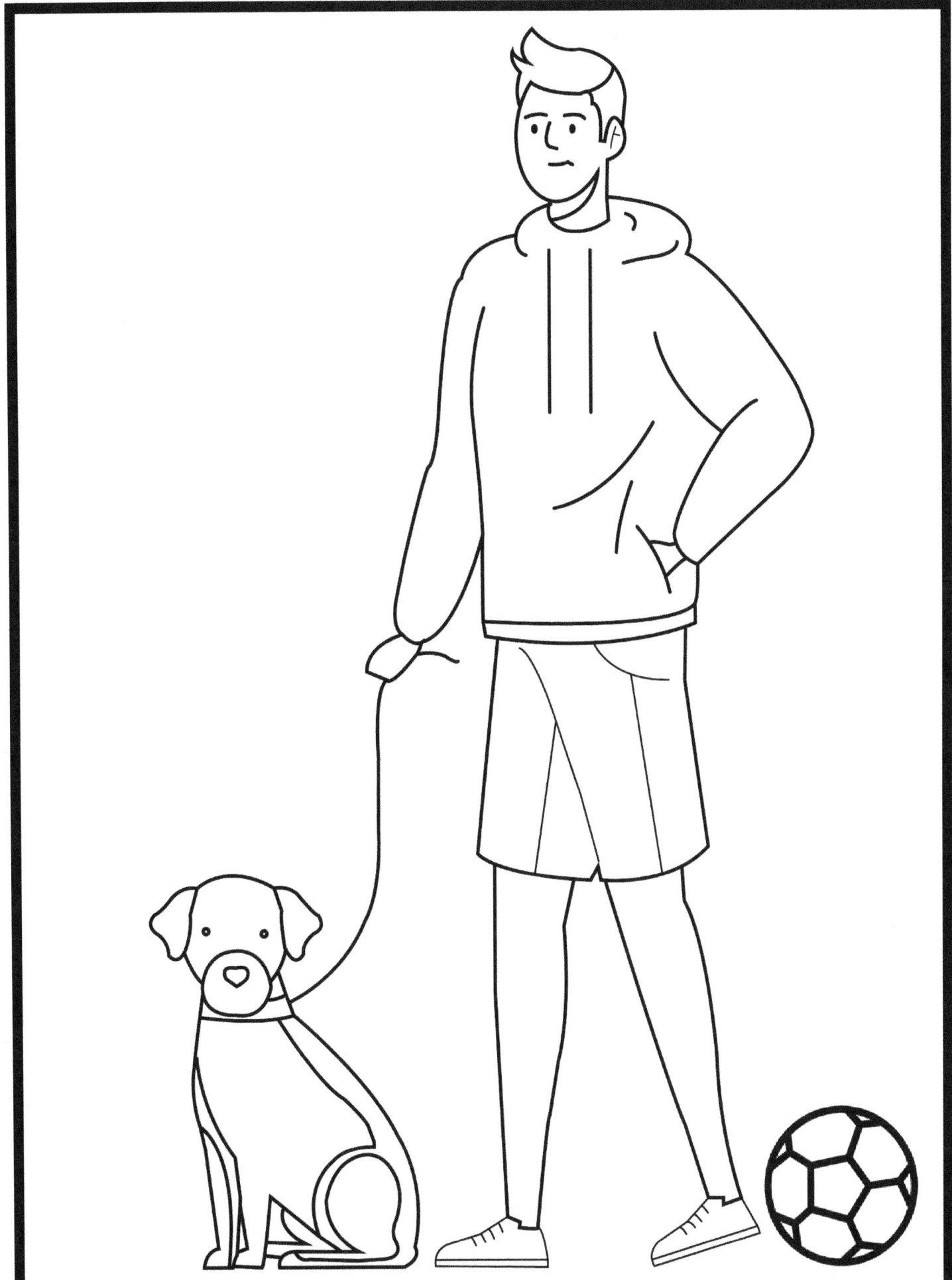

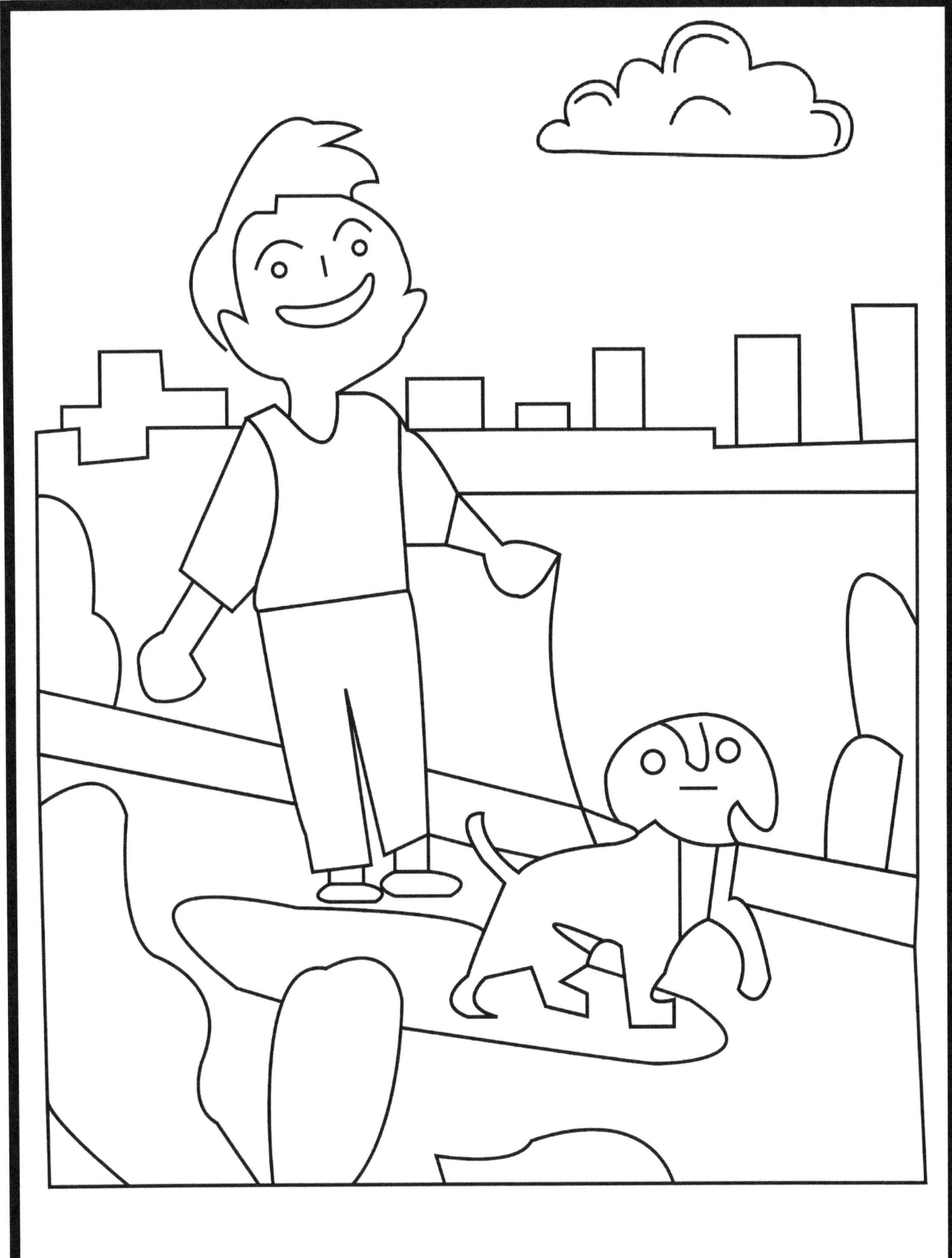

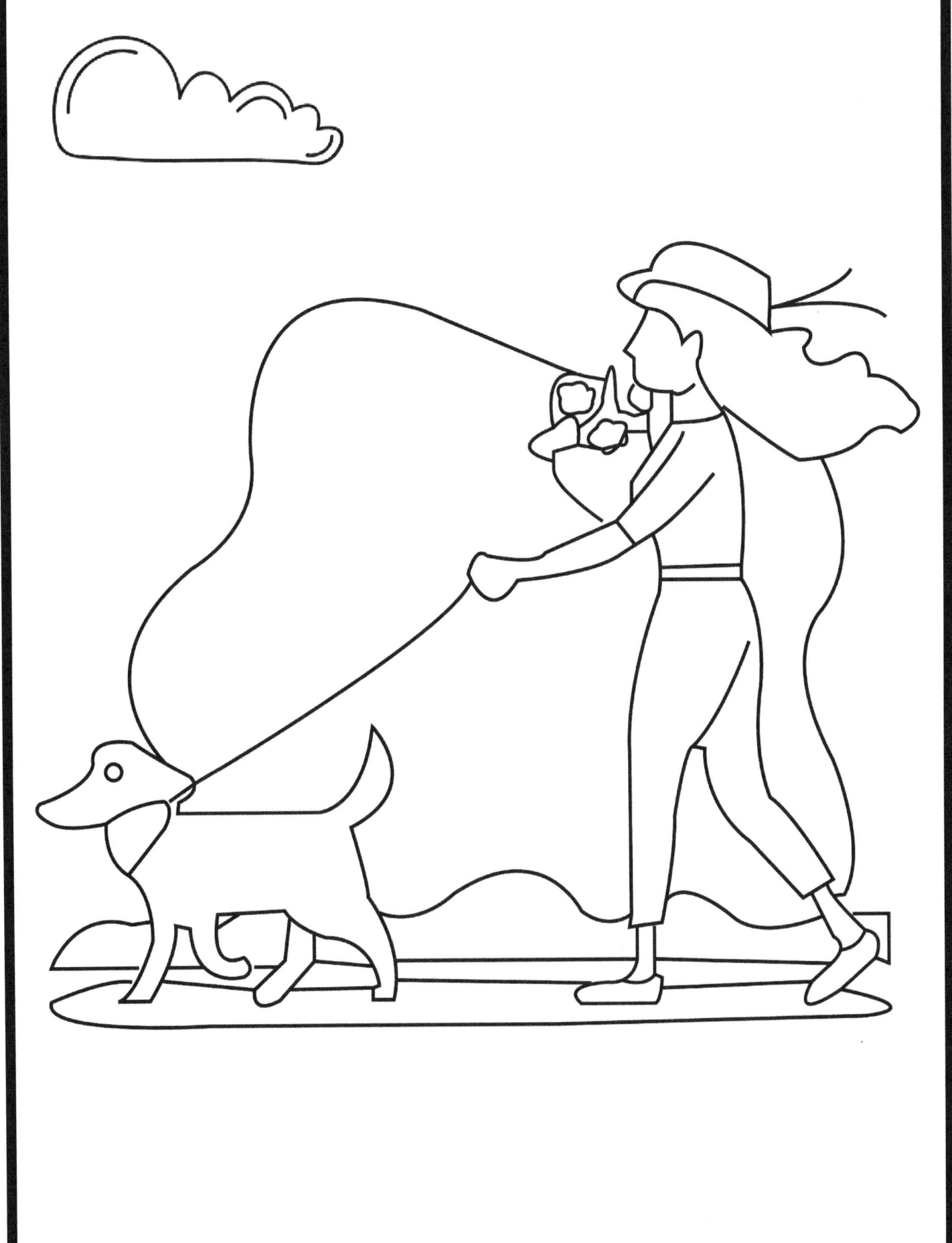

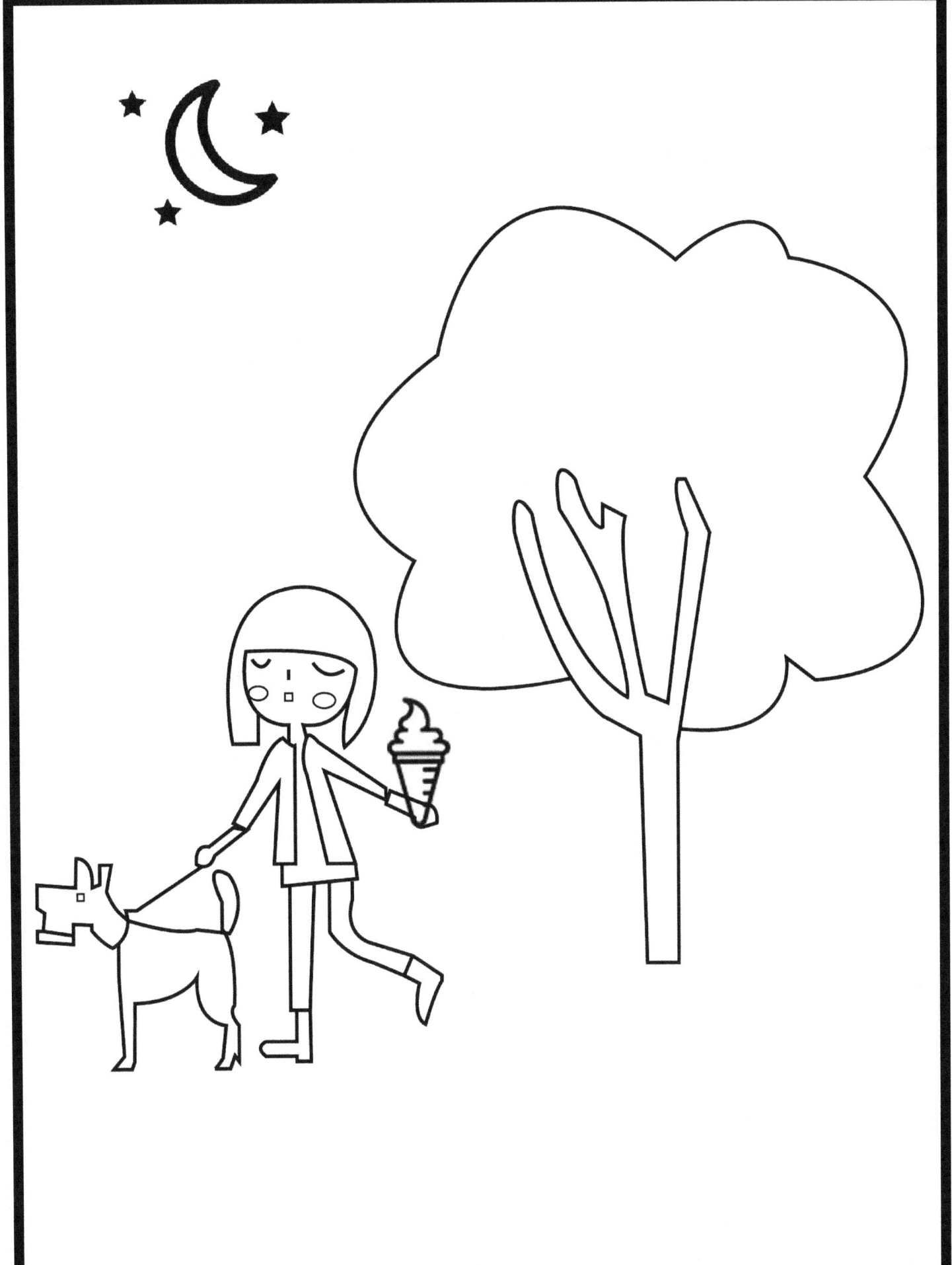

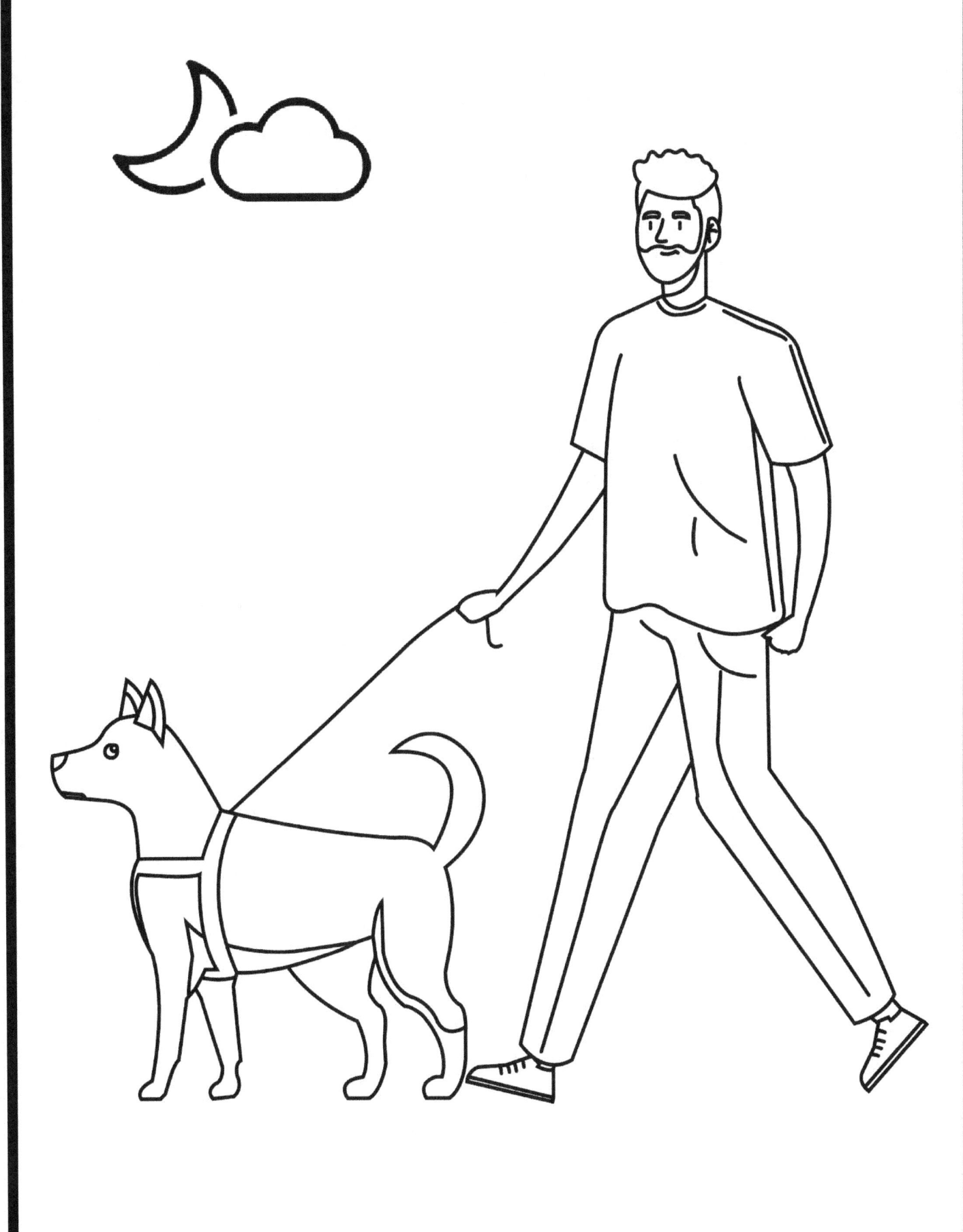

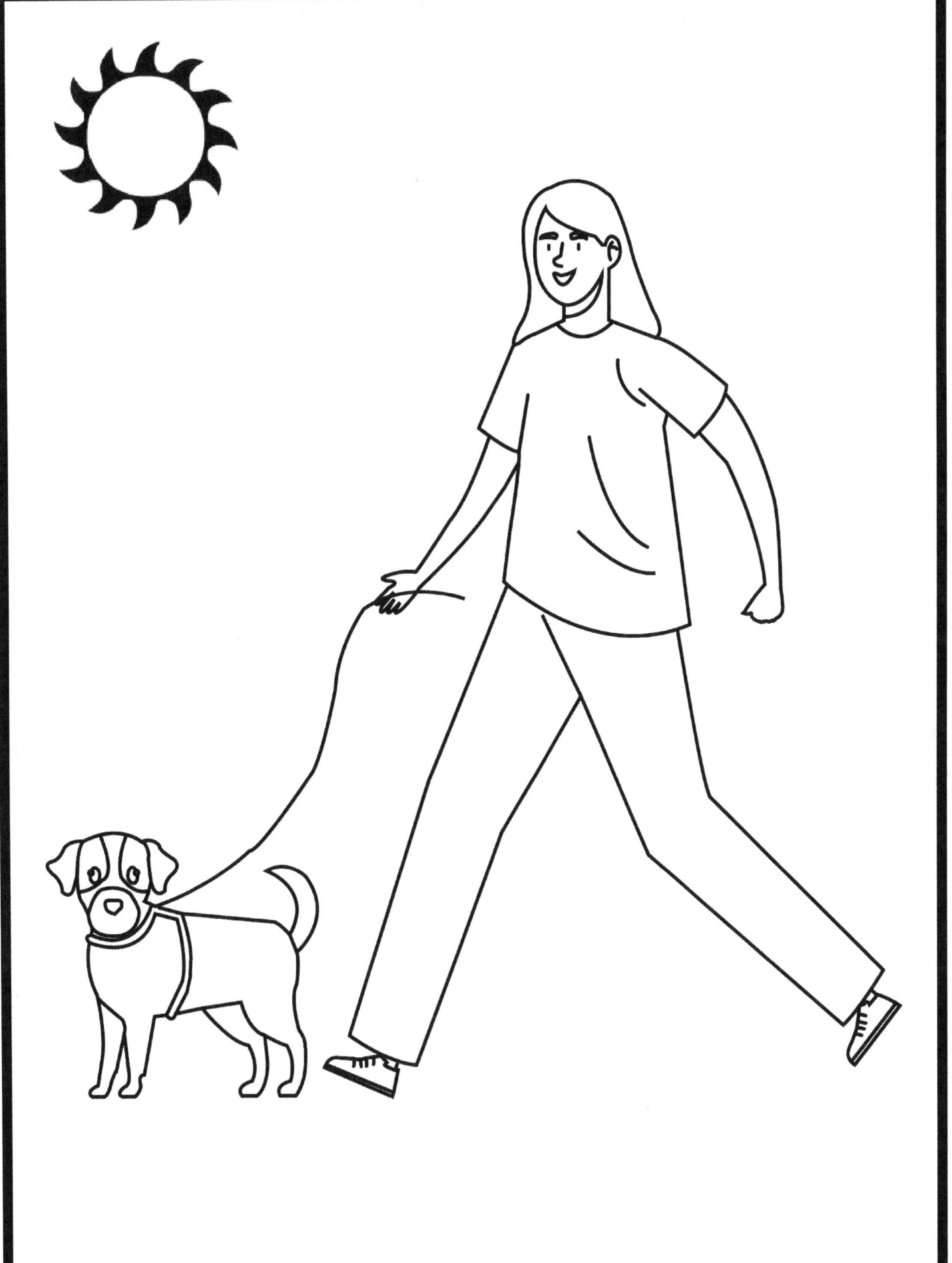

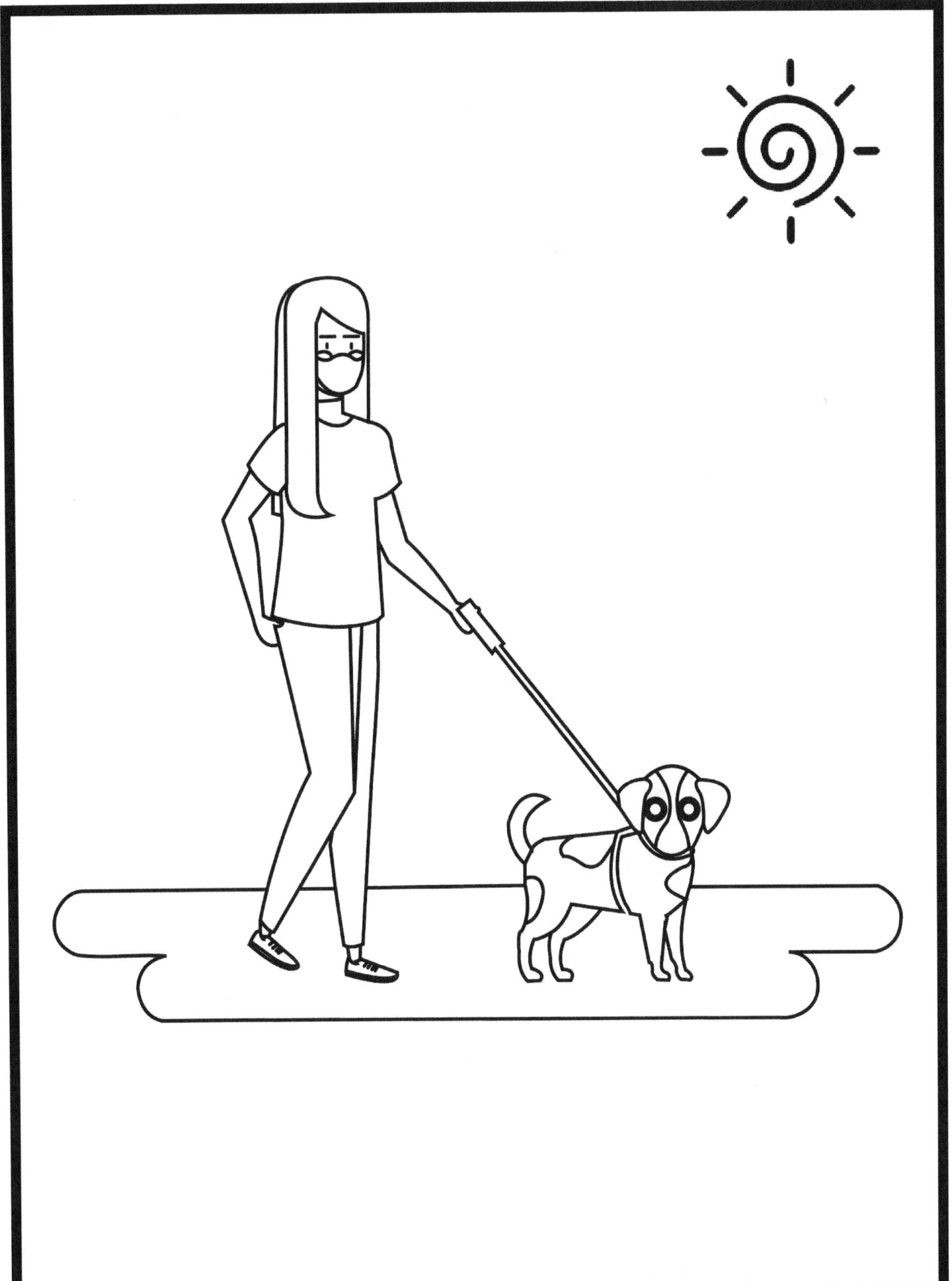

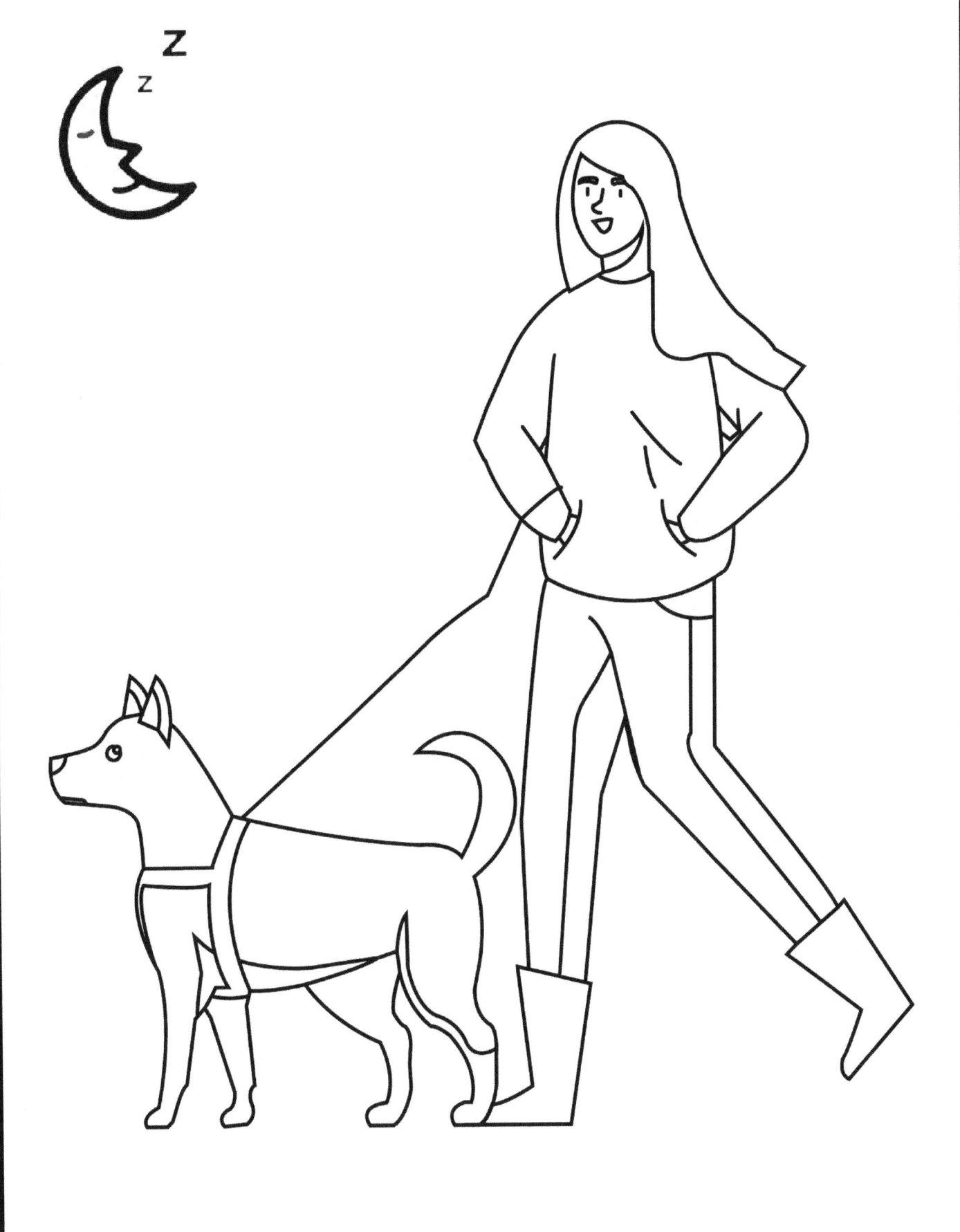

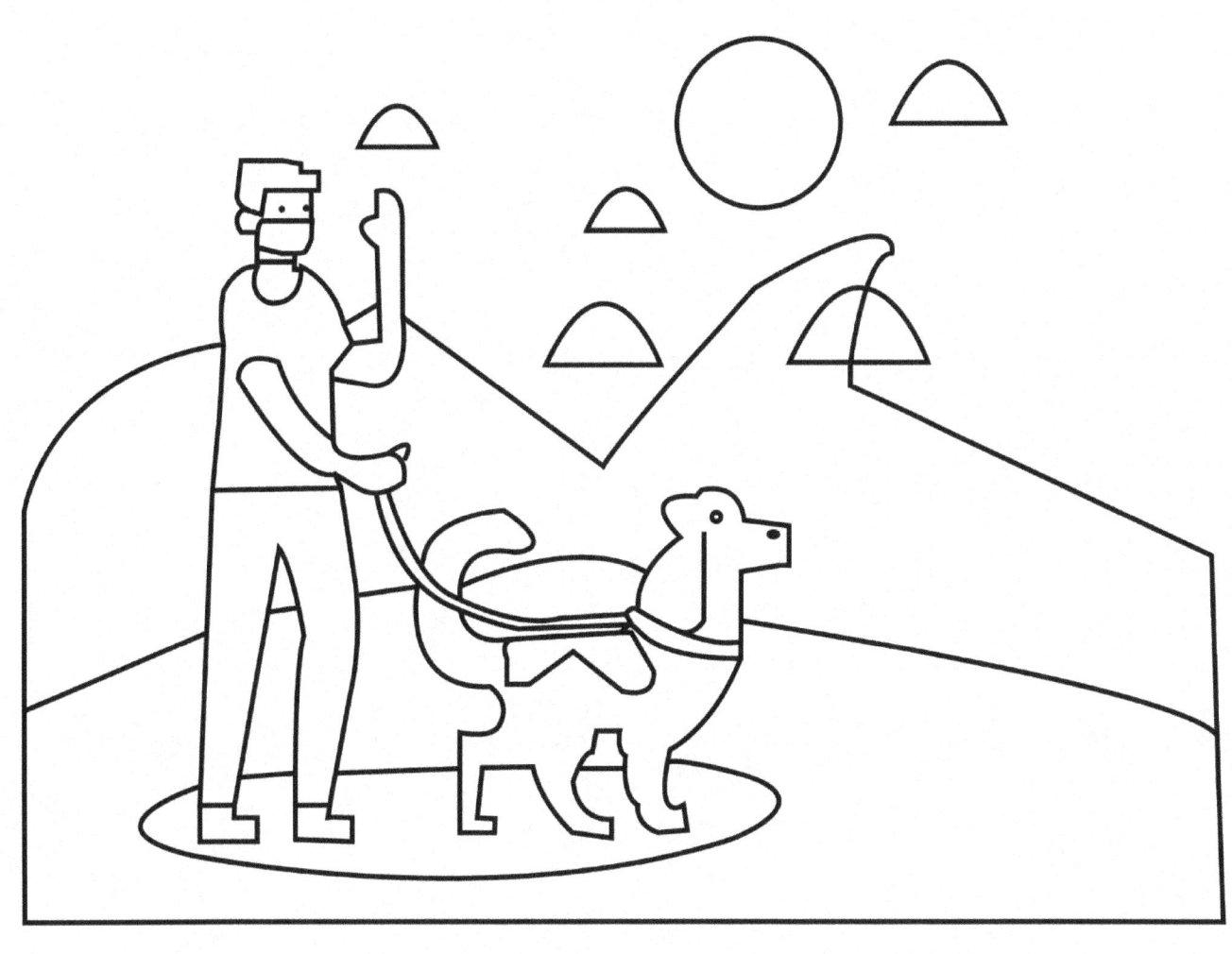

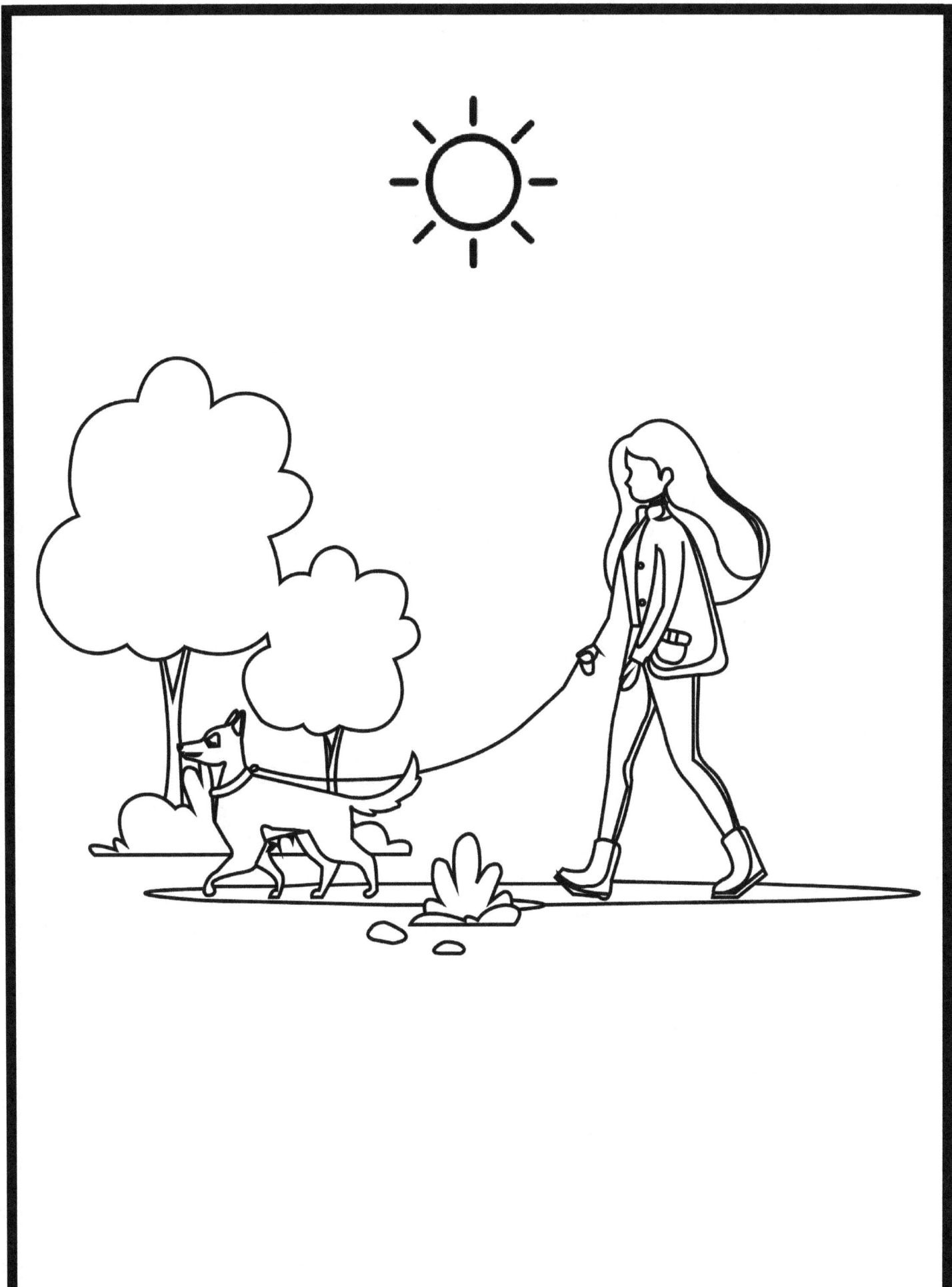

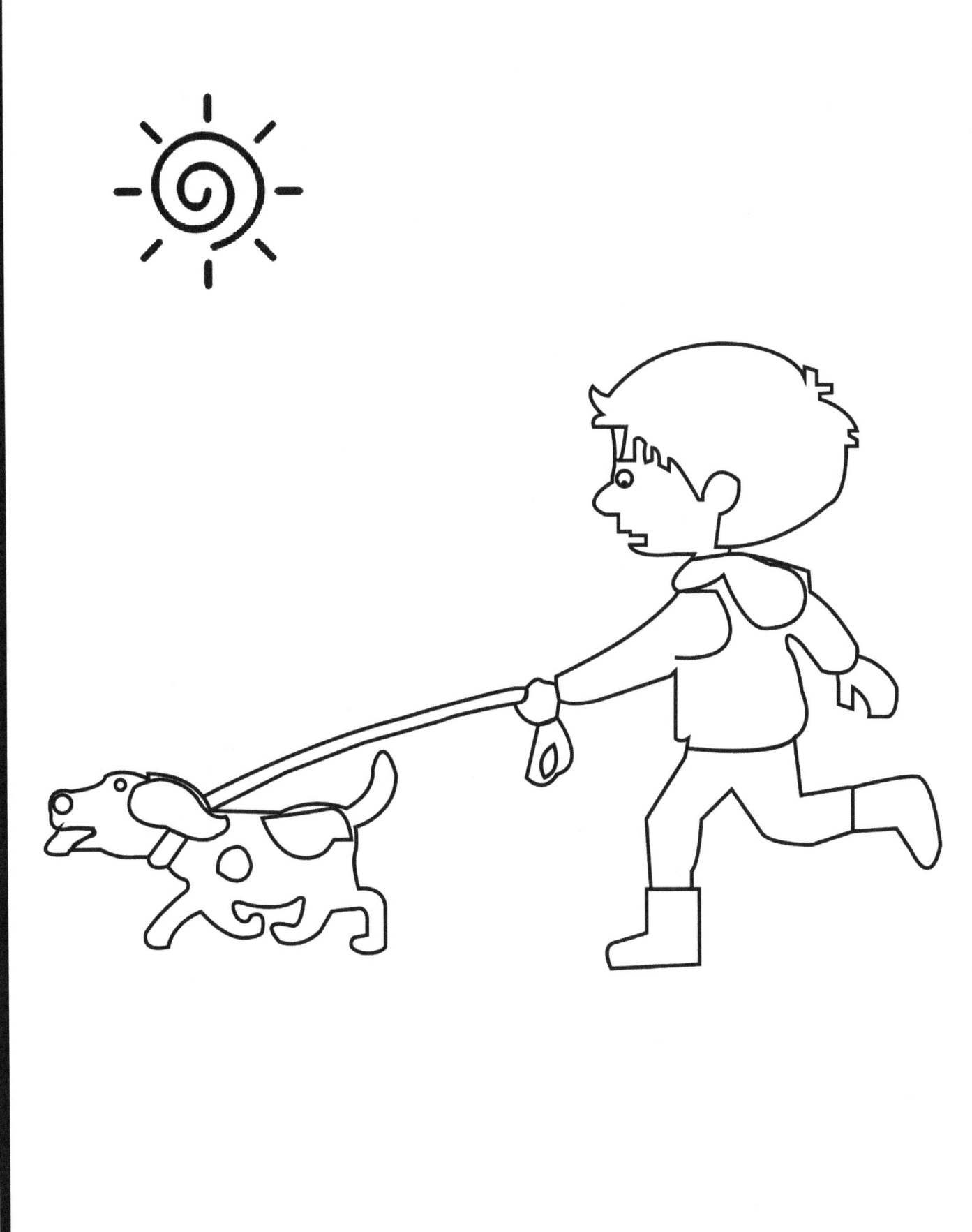

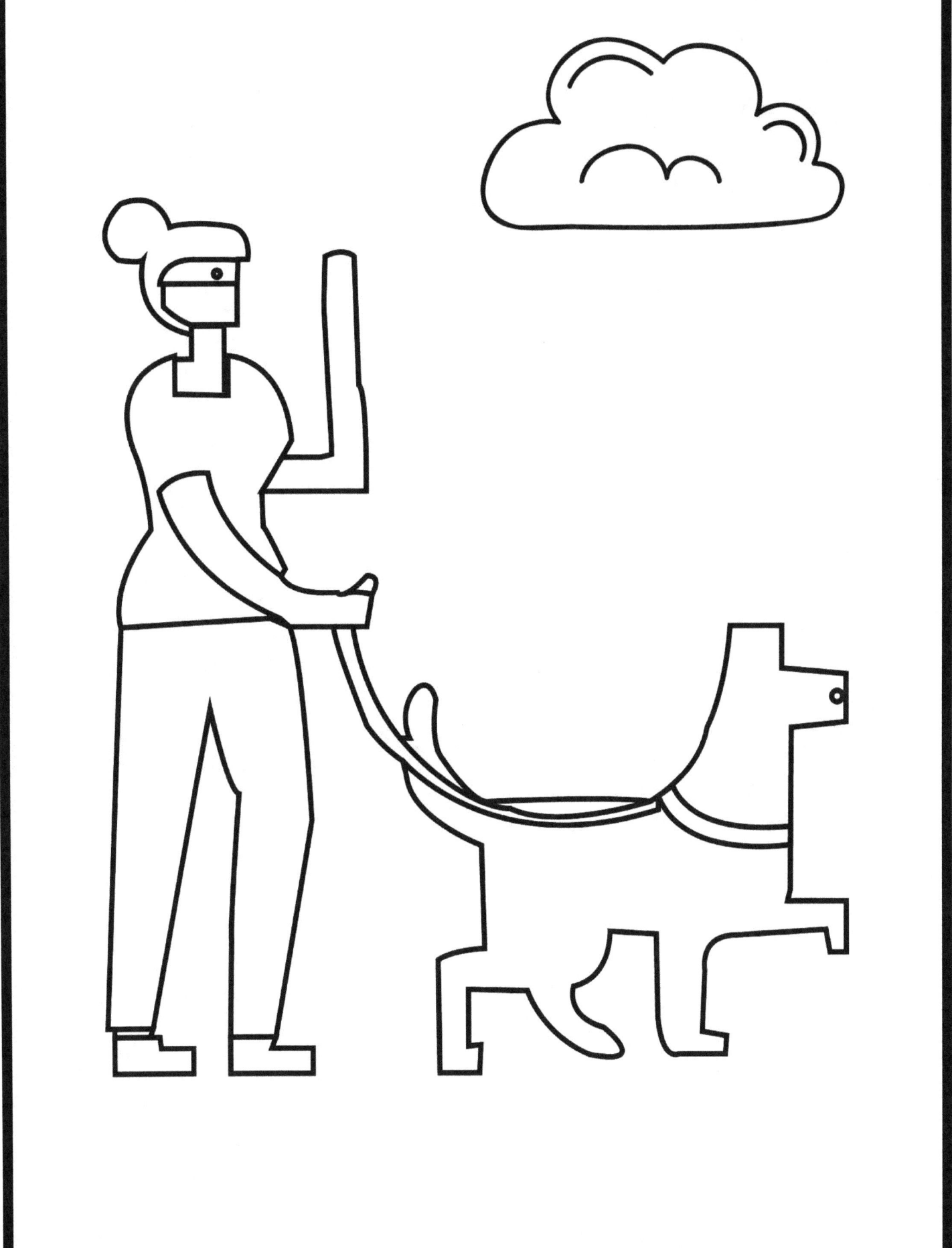

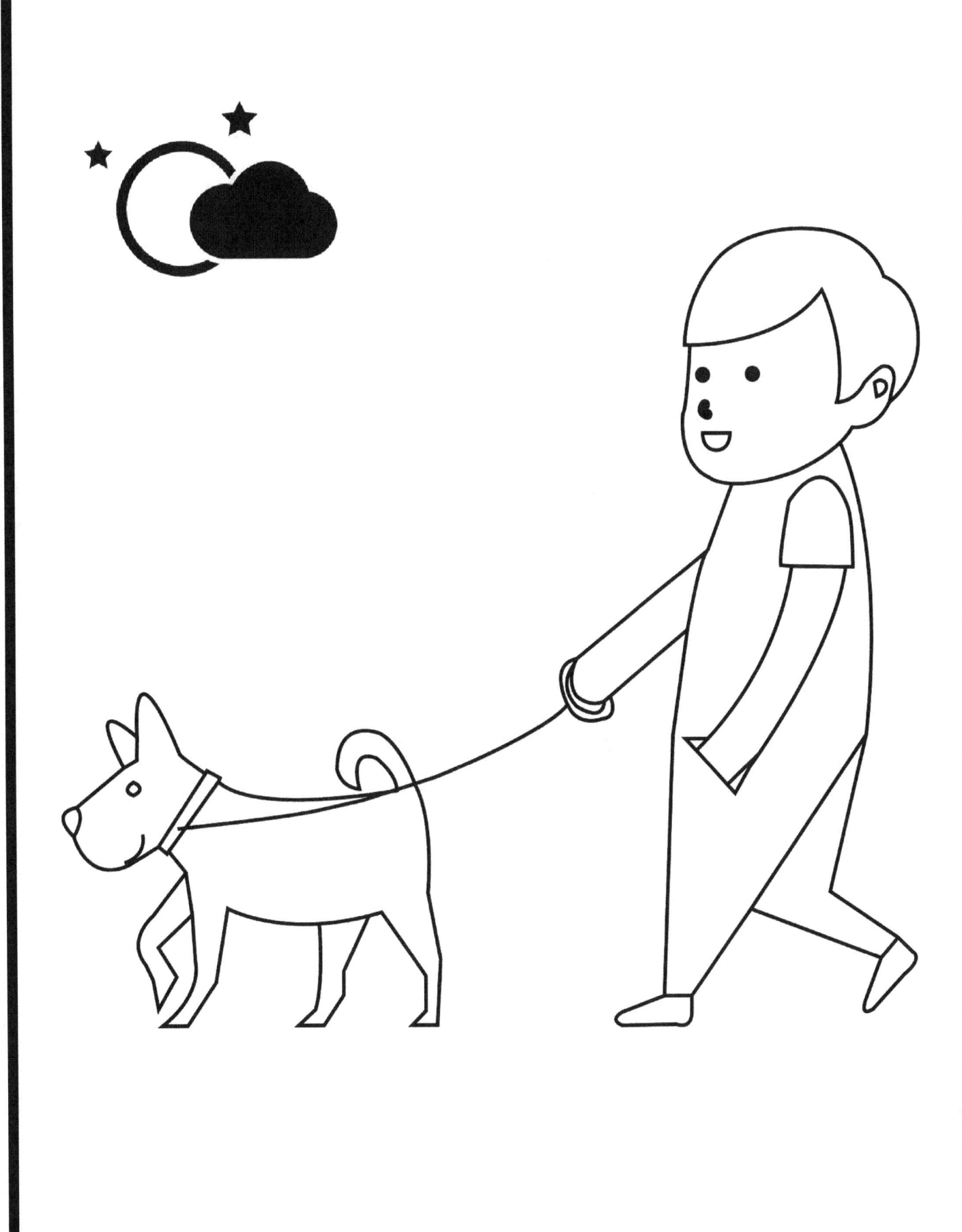

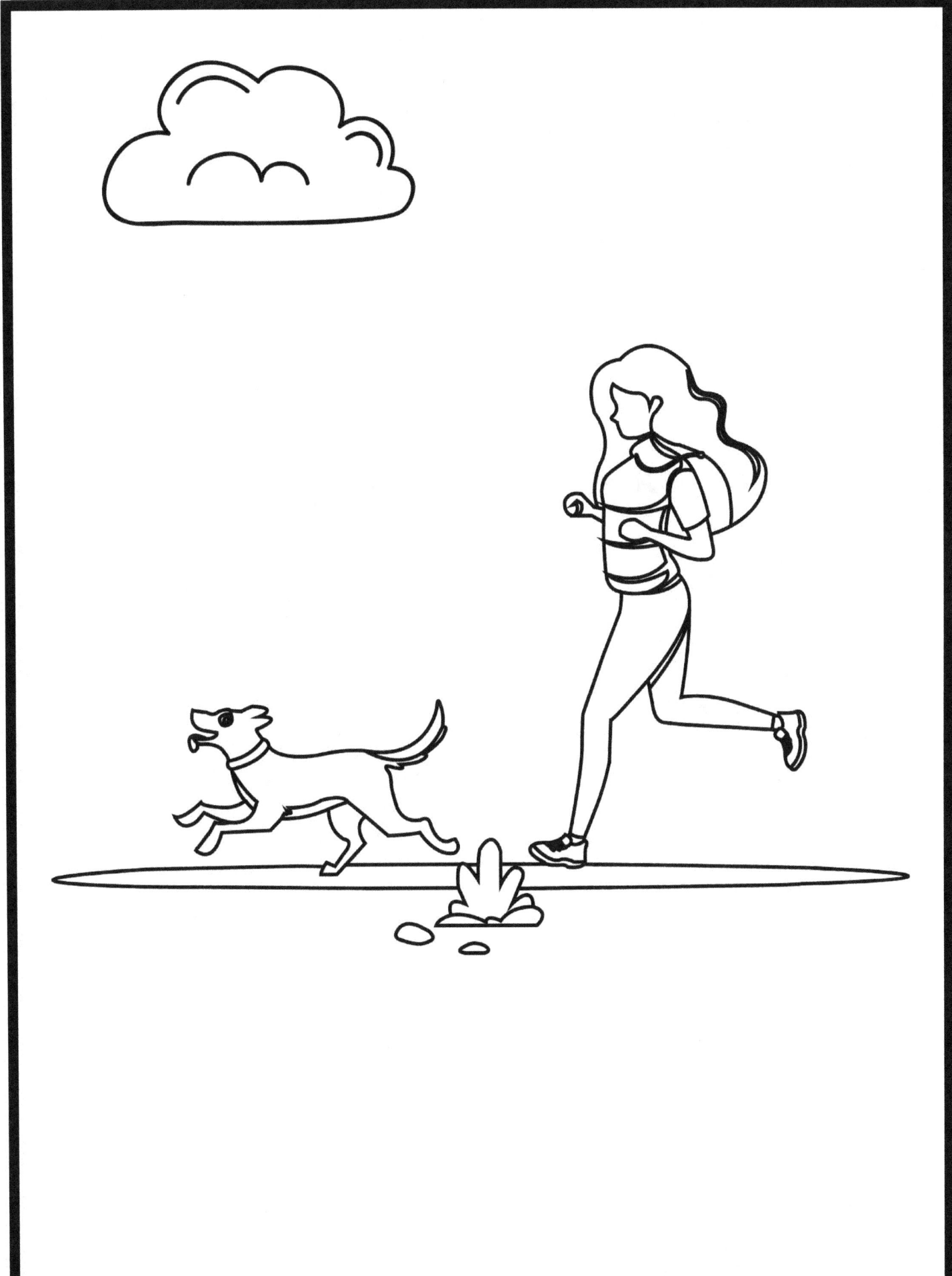

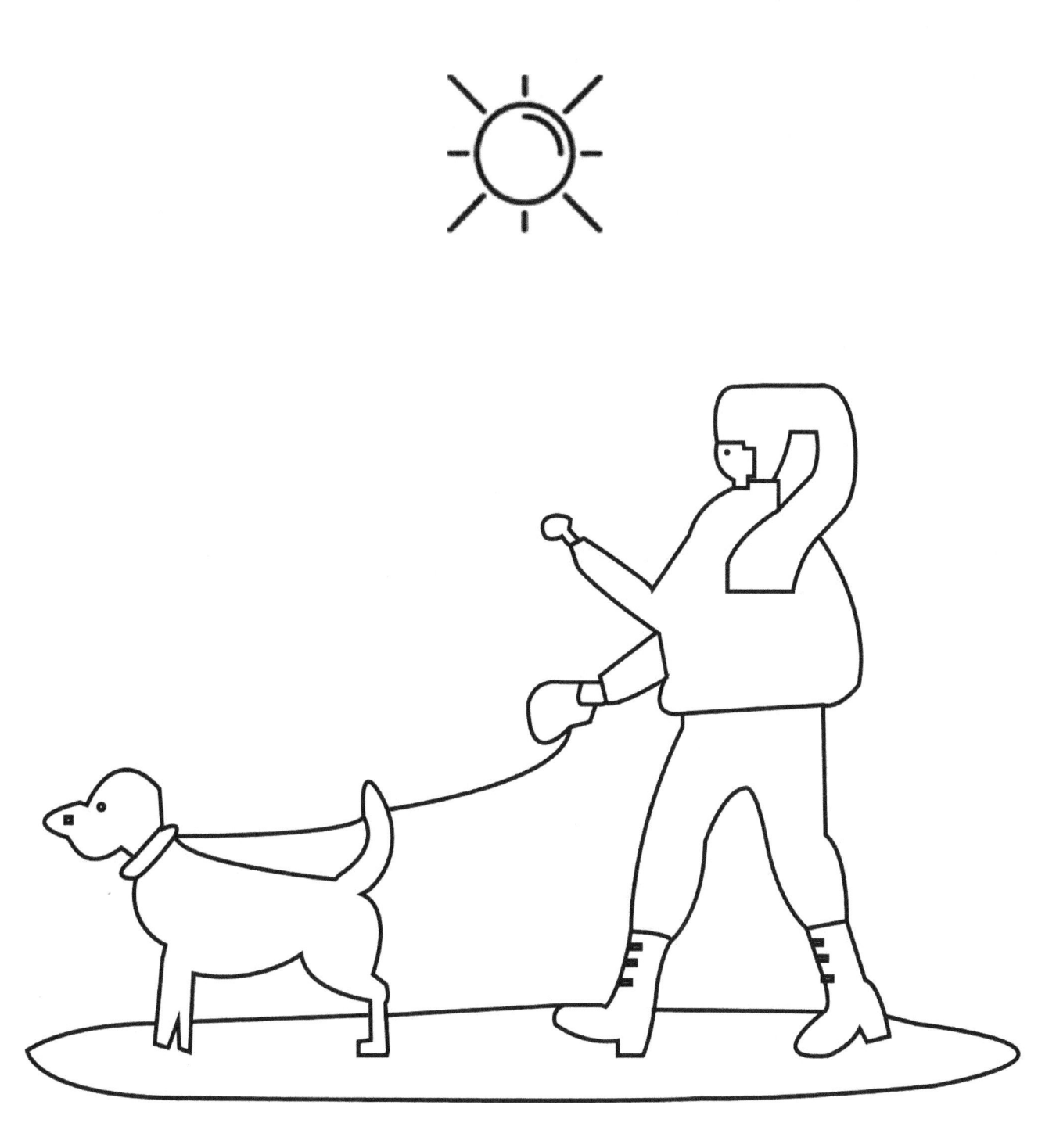

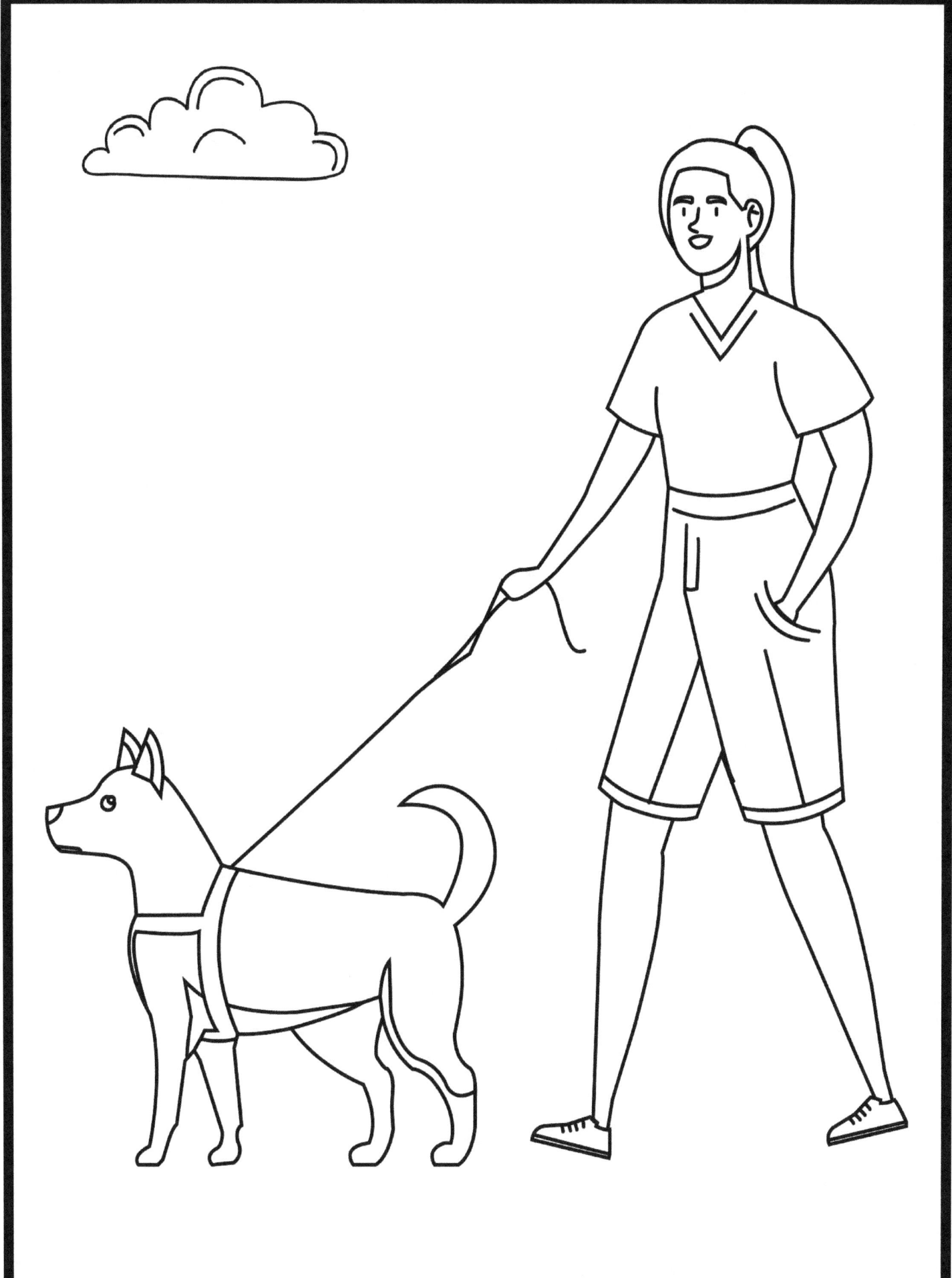

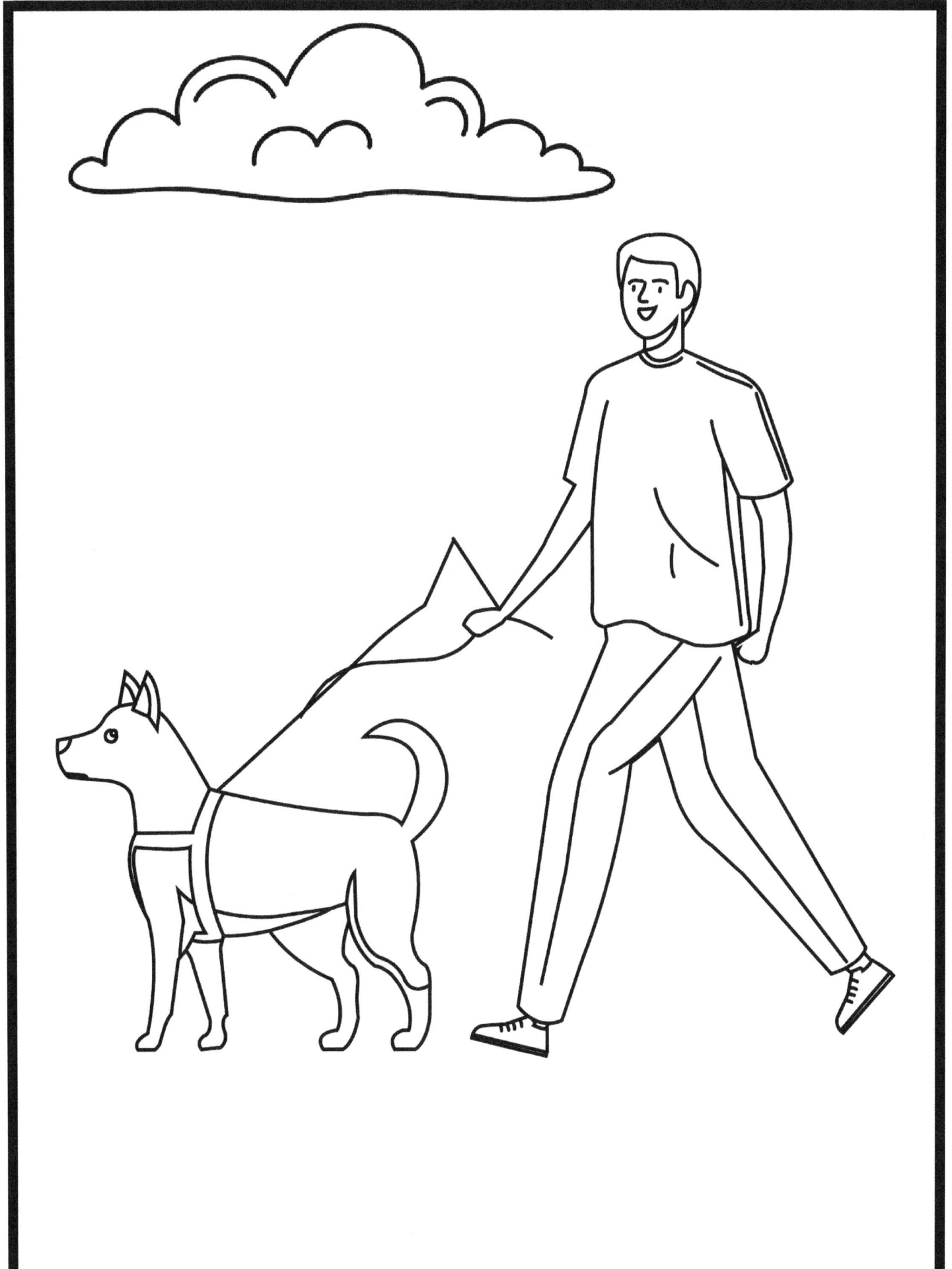

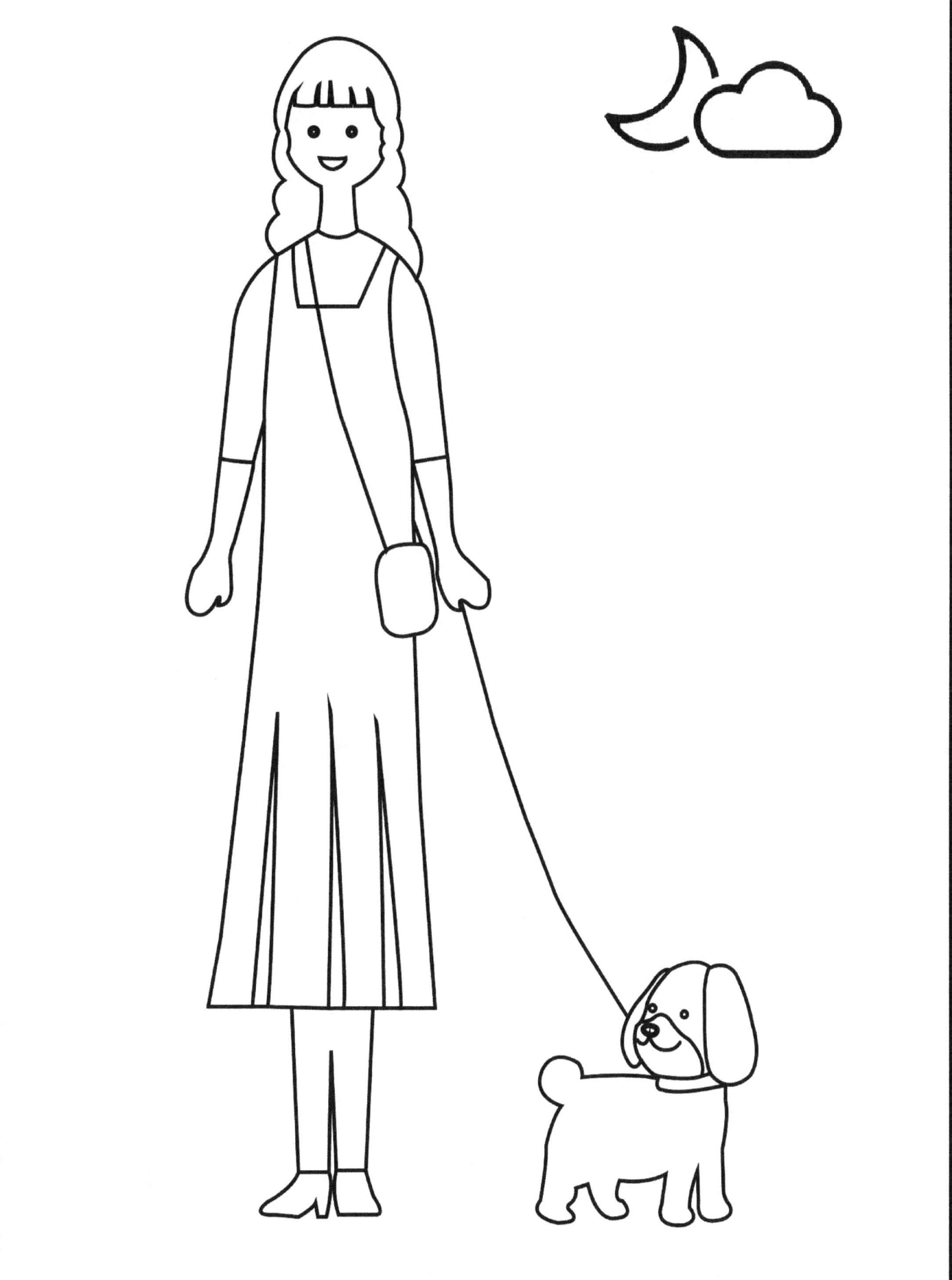

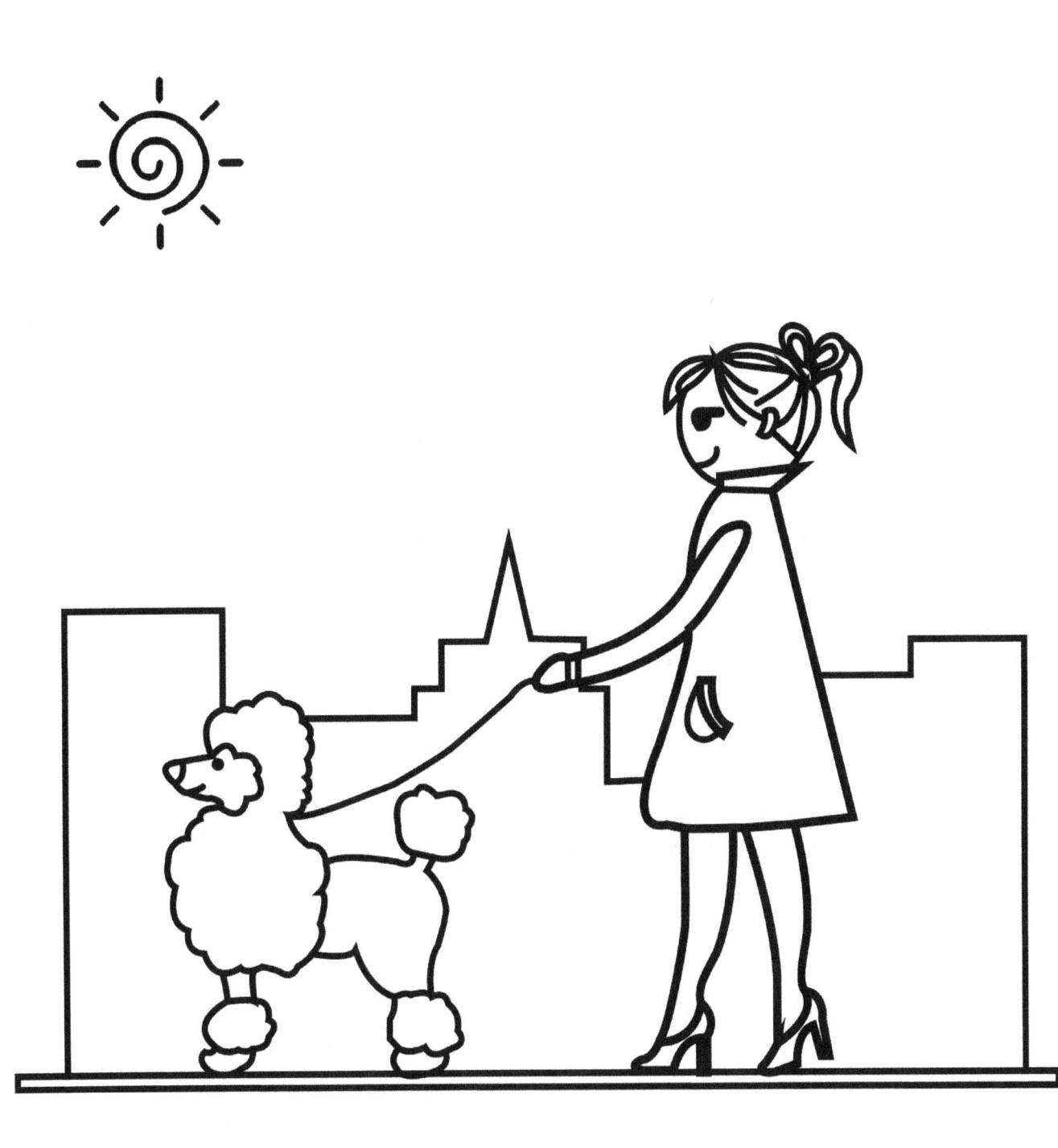

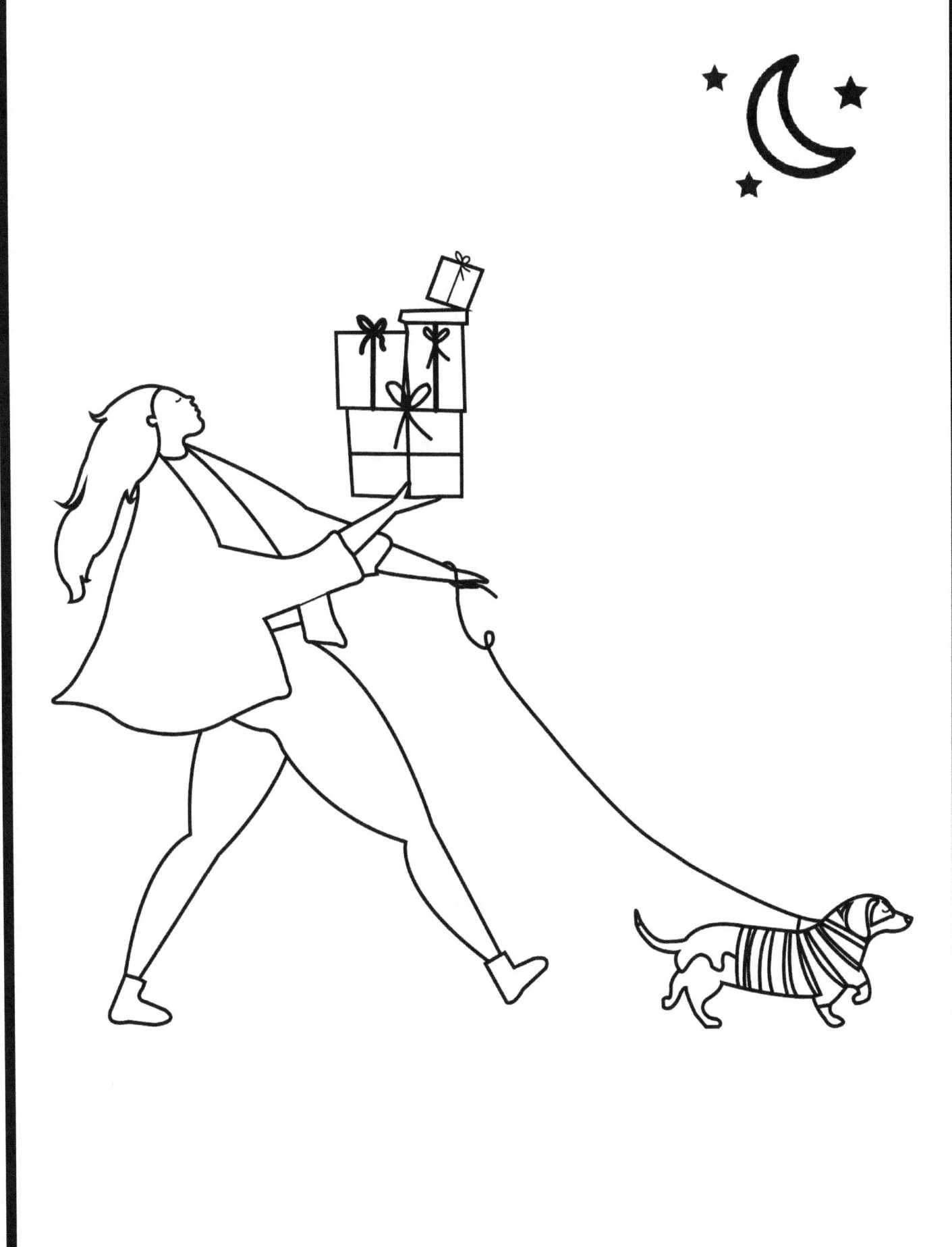

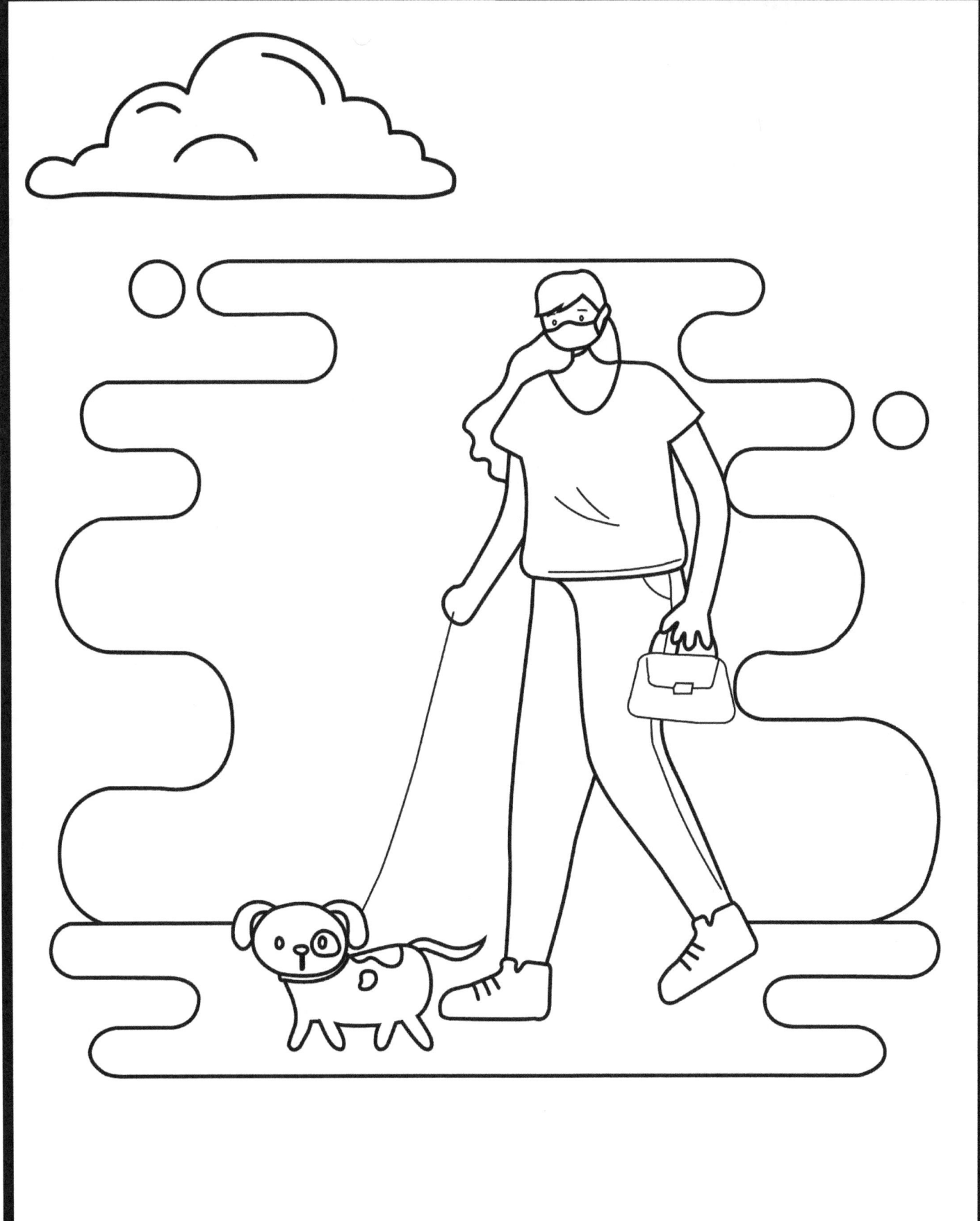

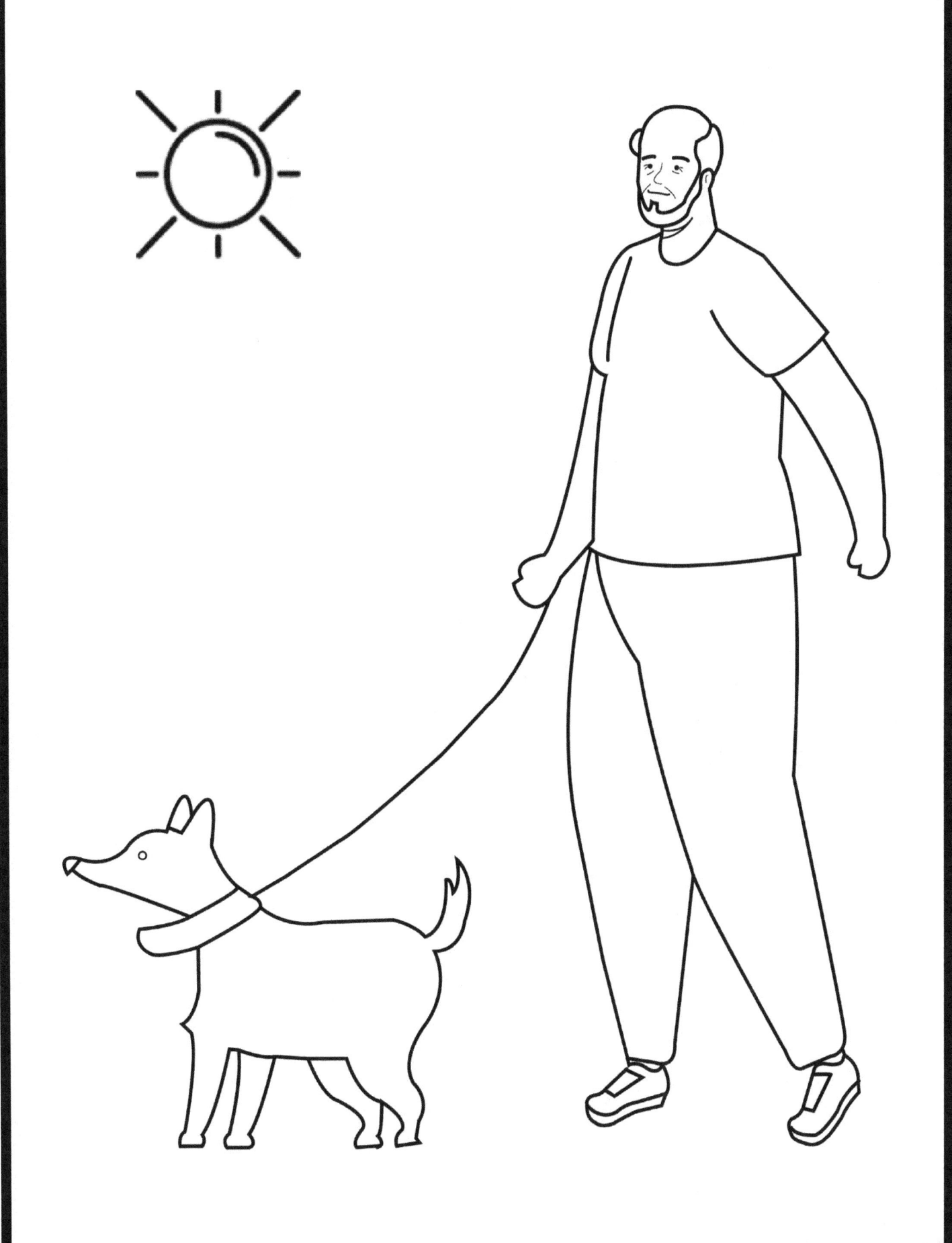

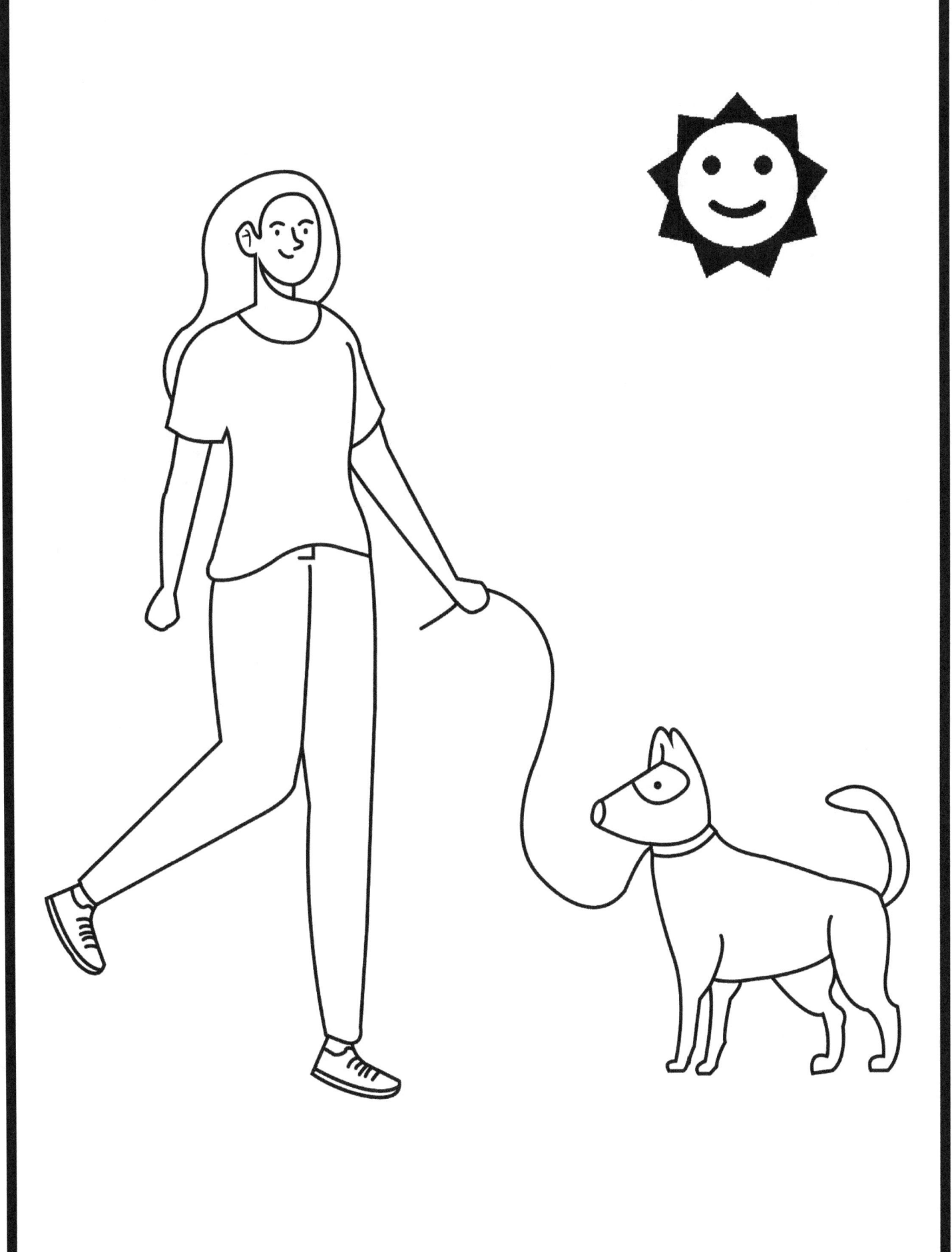

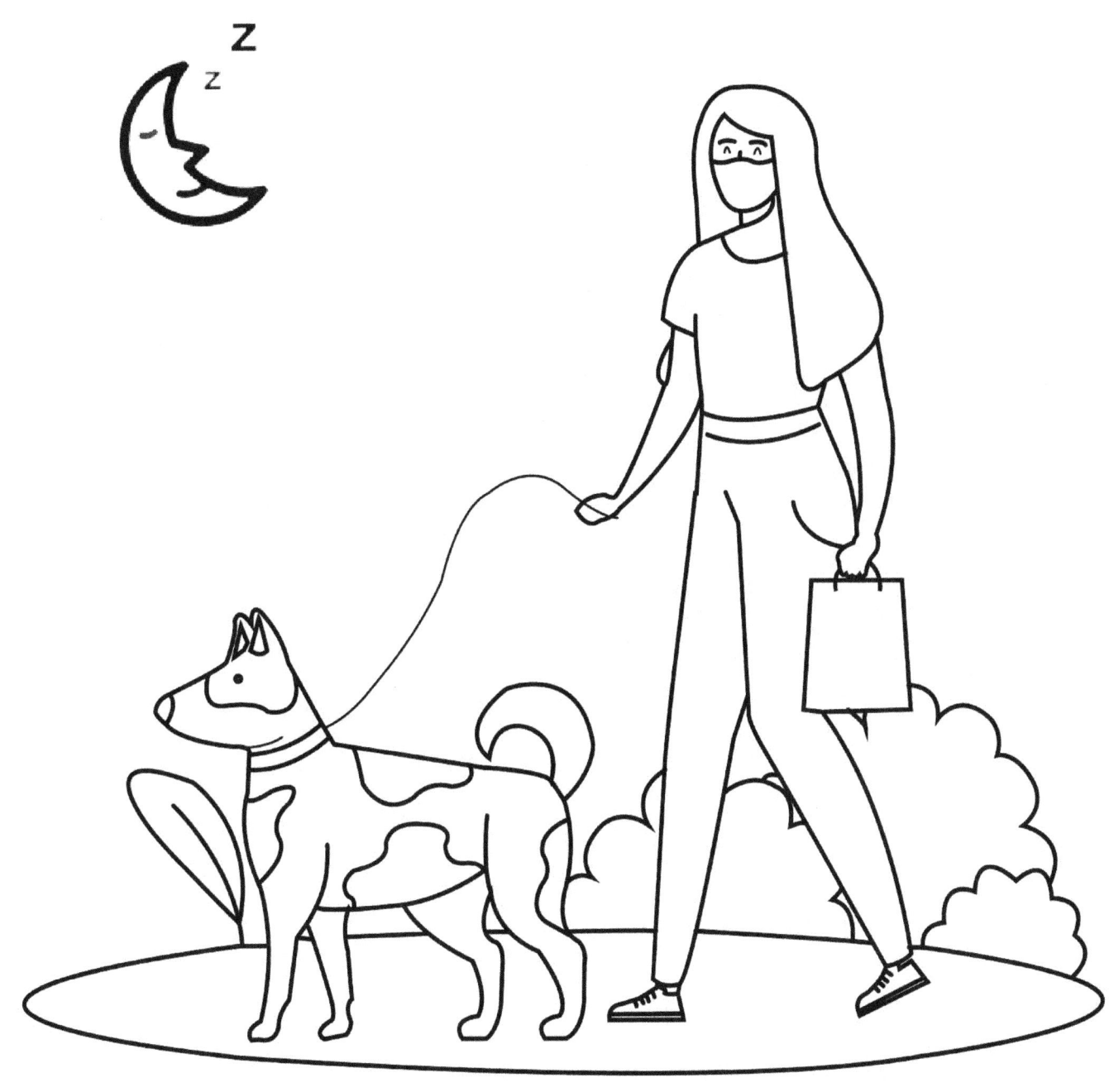

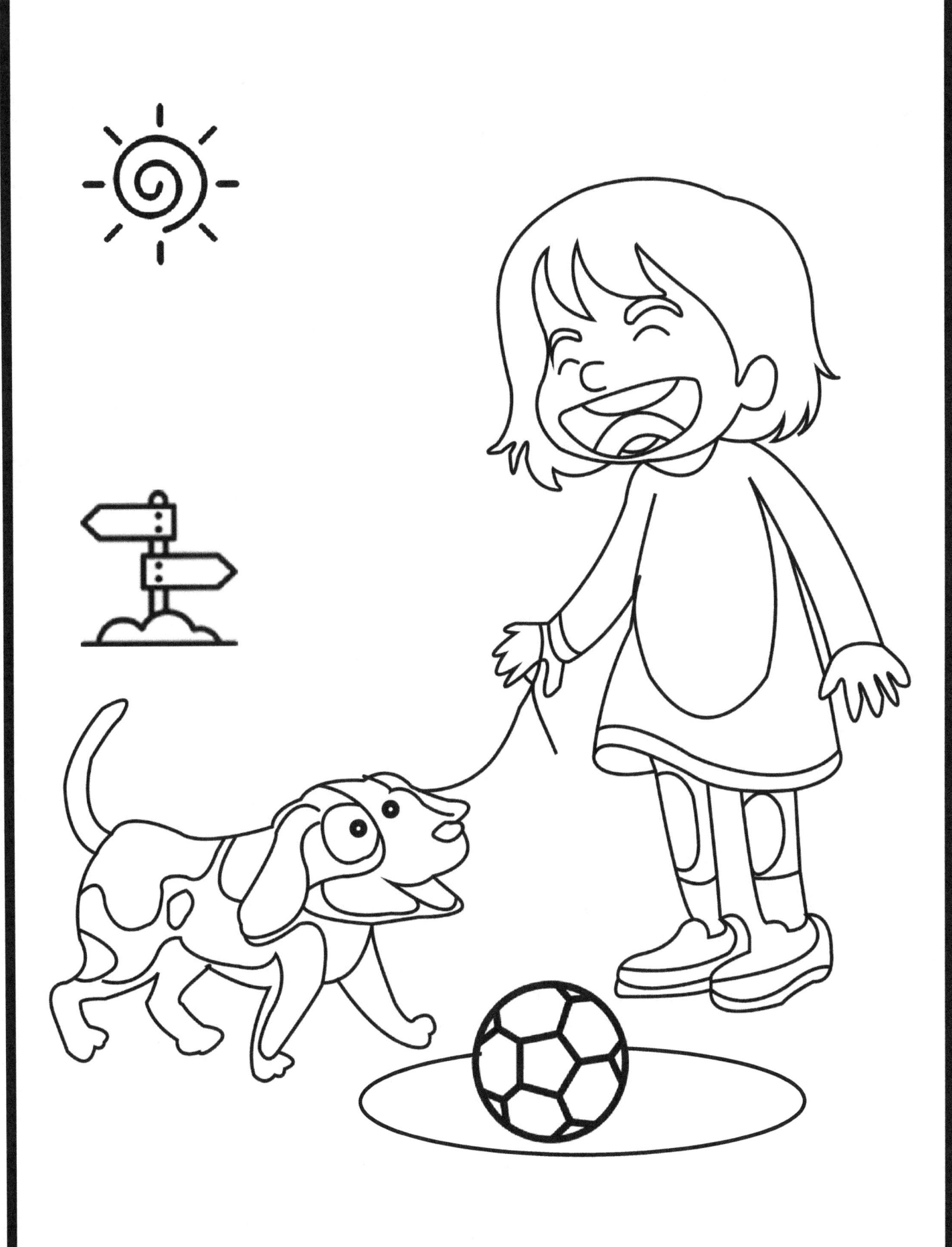

Copyright © 2021 by Chikku Publishing

All rights reserved. No part of this book may be reproduced or used in any manner without written permission of the copyright owner except for the use of quotations in a book review. For more information, visit: https://www.chikkupublishing.com

FIRST EDITION